W9-DDG-259

A Spirituality for Active Ministry

Corita Clarke, R.D.C.

Sheed & Ward

Sheed & Ward™ is a service of National Catholic Reporter Publishing Company, Inc.

Library of Congress Catalog Card Number: 90-61955

ISBN: 1-55612-361-2

Published by: Sheed & Ward
                 115 E. Armour Blvd. P.O. Box 419492
                 Kansas City, MO 64141-6492

To order, call: (800) 333-7373

Contents

Acknowledgements

Many of the issues and questions addressed in this book come from my ministry in teaching, retreat work and spiritual direction. I would like to acknowledge with gratitude all those who have shared their stories of faith and invited me to share part of their spiritual journey.

I am grateful to Reverend Dennis Regan, S.T.D., for his interest, insights and support throughout the process of reflecton and writing. I also want to thank Sister Eileen McKeown, C.S.J., Ph.D., of the Seminary of the Immaculate Conception, and Reverend Richard Woods, O.P., Ph.D., of Loyola University of Chicago, for their suggestions and assistance in preparing the manuscript.

I am also grateful to those who have helped in bringing this manuscript to its completion, Sister Mary Alacoque, R.D.C., and Margaret Gaughan, editorial assistants; Sr. M. Teresa Brady, R.D.C., reader; Marie Flynn, typist; and Sister Mary Kristin, R.D.C., secretarial assistance.

This book is dedicated to the memory of my parents,
Margaret and Joseph
and to my family and friends who have supported
and challenged me along the way.

1
Introduction

A. Context of Ministry

The main context of my ministry is as director of a center for spiritual renewal. Its purpose is to provide opportunities for spiritual growth and renewal for religious and laity, women and men. I am involved in administration, programing, directing retreats, giving workshops and courses, planning liturgical celebrations, and spiritual direction. In addition to this ministry at the center, I also do some teaching in the archdiocesan program in spiritual direction and during the summer I teach in a graduate program in Pastoral Studies in the Midwest. I also serve on the board of directors for an extended renewal program for Christian ministers.

B. Relevance of the Topic

In my ministry I encounter Christian men and women who are engaged in their own search for a viable spirituality, who desire to grow in the lived experience of faith and in discovering its power and relevance in their daily lives. Many of the persons to whom I minister are themselves engaged in some form of ministry in the Church. Many of the questions that surface in my work with these persons, whether in full or part-time ministry, point to the need to search for ways to assist them in exploring the essential components of a contemporary apostolic spirituality and in developing ways to grow in this form of spiritual living in our complex Church and world. This is especially important for those who were formed in a more monastic spirituality of the past, or those who, in more recent times, have received little spiritual formation at all. Many who are theologically astute or even trained for newer aspects of ministry have not been given adequate opportunities for spiritual formation.

C. Purpose of the Book

The main purpose of this book is to develop a guide toward growth in a contemporary spirituality for active ministers. Because of the wide span of topics that this would entail, for the purpose of this book, I will focus on one key issue, the exploration and integration of prayer and action, contemplation and ministry. The goal is to provide a tool for spiritual formation that could be used in a variety of situations: as part of a course in a ministry training program, as an outline for a workshop or a guided retreat, for ongoing discussions in a religious congregation, and as a resource for spiritual directors of those in ministry. The work is envisioned as a resource for the instructor, director or other group leader.

D. Objectives

1. To explore the two main aspects of prayer and action as experienced in contemporary ministerial life. 2. To suggest ways to expand thinking on these two elements and to raise consciousness. 3. To provide reflection questions and activities that could be given to the participants to aid personal integration of the material presented.

E. Method

As we examine the pastoral questions in our lives and try to integrate the various aspects into a meaningful spirituality, I think the first result is the awareness of the complexity of what we are about.

An important contribution from theology that is helpful here is the insistence on the need for theological reflection and more precisely for a method of theological reflection. The two contemporary "giants" in this area of fundamental theology with whom I am most familiar are the late Bernard Lonergan, S.J.[1] and David Tracy[2] of the University of Chicago. In a time of change, challenge and crisis such as ours, when the theological pursuit of "faith seeking understanding" is intensified, theologians are challenged—in David Tracy's words—to "a successful articulation"[3] of the Christian vision which can give meaning to our common life.

In the quest for a spirituality for ministry, the need is for a method of practical theology, or pastoral theological reflection. A method of pastoral reflection invites us to ask such questions as: "Where is God in this situation?" "Where are we being called now?" It can lead us not only to understanding and insight, but also to pastoral action. As Charles Gerkin has stated, the goal of practical theology is the "transformation of life in all its dimensions in accordance with the Christian gospel."[4]

Upon reflection, I have come to realize that the method elaborated by James and Evelyn Whitehead is the one that provides the richest resource for reflection for me. In *Method in Ministry*,[5] drawing on the work of Lonergan, Tracy and others, the Whiteheads offer a model and a method that involves:

1. Attending—to the three main resources for pastoral reflection: the Christian tradition, personal experience, and information from the contemporary culture.

2. Assertion—a process of clarification and challenge that results from the correlation of these three sources of information.

3. Decision—which flows from a new perspective and leads to action.

In subsequent chapters I have followed this model for reflection, and invite those using this book into their own process of pastoral theological reflection. The Appendix develops some of the important foundational insights of both Lonergan and Tracy, and describes in more detail the elements of the Whiteheads' method of pastoral theological reflection. I encourage those for whom further explanation would be helpful to refer to this part of the book.

2

A Description of the Key Concepts

A. Spirituality and Spiritual Life

Spirituality, like the Spirit and the reality it expresses, is hard to pin down, to define or to institutionalize. Spirituality is concerned with the search for the transcendent dimension of life and with the manner of living that flows from its apprehension. Our Christian expression of spirituality is our life lived in awareness of the gift of the Spirit received at our baptism into Christ, and in response to this Spirit of God active in us as energy and presence. The presence of God is the Spirit of Jesus who teaches us and draws us with Jesus to the Father. Because of the Incarnation, all that has to do with human living can be relevant for a spiritual life.

Spirituality is both personal and also rooted in the shared experience of a tradition. A contemporary spirituality involves appropriating the vision for our human lives today and living out that vision in the power of the Spirit. It requires sensitive listening to the leading of the Spirit, both within our own hearts and in the manifold expressions of God's Presence in our life and in our world. David Knight has expressed the insight that "The spiritual life begins when a person realizes that there is something going on between themselves and God, and they choose to be involved in that." In this view, a spiritual life involves both *awareness* and *positive response*.

B. Religious Experience

Key to our comprehension of spirituality is the awareness of God and God's intervention in our lives which can be called religious experience.

By this term I do not mean to designate only unusual or phenomenal experiences in persons' lives, but rather any experience in which one can perceive the possibility of the divine, or which is in Karl Rahner's expression, a "signal of transcendence." Rahner's approach to spirituality through a Christian anthropology is very helpful in describing religious experience. For Rahner, God is Mystery, "Holy Mystery," and "the human person is of his essence he who must lose himself in loving Mystery."[1] This is possible only because of God's Self-communication. ". . . our whole life is orientated to a loving, forgiving Mystery, which is the basis of our existence. God is the loving, holy Mystery whose historical Self-communication has reached its high point in Jesus Christ and become radically interior through the sending of the Holy Spirit."[2]

Rahner views the human person as "the universal question"[3] and the Christian message as the source of the answer to this question. Because of the question at the core of each person, there is also the possibility of recognizing the Self-communication of God. In a powerfully crafted statement, Rahner has indicated how this revelation of God can be experienced in seemingly ordinary human life. He enumerates "signals of transcendence" such as the experience of loneliness, of forgiveness without expecting reward, of fidelity to the depths of one's conscience; of faithfulness, hope, love, even when there are no apparent reasons; the experience of the gap between what we desire and what we receive from life; hope in the face of death.[4] Through the human capacity for reflection on one's experience, and the ever-present gift of God's grace, the ordinary moments of life contain the potential of revealing God's presence.

One of the tasks of ministry is to assist people to be open to the presence of God in their lives and not to miss the true religious experience of life itself. This book will invite ministers to engage in precisely this kind of reflection.

C. Discipleship

The Self-communication of God of which Rahner wrote is most clear and visible for the Christian in Jesus. The vocation to Christianity is a call that comes in baptism to know and follow Jesus in discipleship. Discipleship as presented in the New Testament is an invitation to intimacy: to come close to Jesus at his invitation, to learn from being with him how to live in relationship not only to him, but also to his Father, and to all others, and to be sent out by Jesus, missioned for the sake of the gospel. The grace of discipleship demands attentive following of Jesus and radical commitment to his Person, his values and his mission for the coming of the Kingdom or the Reign of God.

A contemporary spirituality for Christian ministry must be grounded in the knowledge and love of Jesus Christ. This implies knowledge of the Scripture, especially the Gospels. It is a knowledge of the heart that comes not only by study, but even more through prayerful contemplation of Jesus' life and message. The challenge of the spiritual life is to live as Jesus' disciple in one's own time, in such a way as to invite others to respond to his call, to "go make disciples." (Matt. 28:19)

In this category of discipleship Avery Dulles, S.J., finds what he has described as an appropriate model of the Church for our time. In addition to his original five models, Dulles has suggested a sixth model of the Church as "a community of disciples." In this model, the Church is the people who are called together, gathered in, but the Church is also those who are sent out, missioned.

D. Mission and Ministry for the Kingdom

Christian ministry originates in the mission and ministry of Jesus. Jesus' mission was his involvement in God's plan for the world, his loving concern and care for the salvation of everyone. Jesus' ministry was his compassionate, loving service that assisted in the fulfillment of God's plan, the coming of God's Kingdom. In the synoptic Gospels Jesus announces the inauguration of this Kingdom, and in Luke he describes his involvement in the coming of that Kingdom with the reading of the scroll of the prophet Isaiah, where he identifies with the prophet. He describes how this Reign of God will become visible, through his ministry of compassion. (Luke 4:16-21)

Through baptism all Christians are called to ministry, to continue the mission of Jesus through lives of witness and service which promote the coming of the reign of God in their own time. The *Decree on the Apostolate of the Laity* from the Second Vatican Council makes it clear that this apostolic involvement is as essential for the laity as it is for those in the religious life or clergy (a. 3, 13, 37). Therefore, the search for a contemporary spirituality for active ministry cannot have a narrow focus nor be delineated for an elite minority in the Church. An apostolic spirituality is one that forms the foundation for active involvement in bringing the message of the gospel to the world. As George Aschenbrenner, S.J., has stated succinctly:

> In the sense of serious commitment to and involvement with our world, every disciple of Jesus must be intensely apostolic. Not to be apostolic, in this sense, is simply to betray Christian discipleship.[5]

For Aschenbrenner, even monastic spirituality must thus be apostolic, e.g., through concern and prayer for the world, so the term active apostolic spirituality is a clearer delineation for the purpose of this study.

The question "Is there a different spirituality for active members of religious communities and clergy and another for lay persons?" is raised frequently today. It is my conviction that there is one gospel spirituality of discipleship that is to be lived out in different life-styles. That is an underlying presupposition in looking at spirituality in this book.

E. Relationship of the Church and the World

Since the Second Vatican Council's *Dogmatic Constitution on the Church in the Modern World* proclaimed that "The joys and the hopes, the griefs and the anxieties of the men of this age, especially those who are poor or in any way afflicted, these too are the joys and hopes, the griefs and anxieties of the followers of Christ" (a.1), the concept of ministry to the world has taken on a new emphasis. The Council expressed the renewed vision of the world as the arena of God's activity. There was a breaking down of the separation of the secular and the sacred, which had been inherited along with many other forms of dualism from far back in the history of the Church through platonic philosophy. A spirituality of ministry today flows from the responsibility to manifest God's presence *in* the world. The challenge offered to the laity by the Council is to be the leaven, to bring the gospel message into all aspects of human life, into the marketplace. It is in the everyday experience of men and women that the Reign of God is coming. This progress of the Kingdom in the world and in the hearts of people is the mission of the Church, and it is the mission underlying all aspects of ministry. Jesus sent his disciples into the world, but he also prayed that they would not be of the world (John 17:14-19). It is in this challenge to speak meaningfully to the contemporary world, yet to take a countercultural stance toward much that is of the world, that many of the questions surrounding contemporary spirituality arise.

F. Contemporary Cultural Context of the United States

Ministry in the contemporary United States Church faces a unique cultural setting, and the importance of this factor for spirituality cannot be overemphasized. As David Lonsdale, S.J. has indicated:

> . . . all spirituality is rooted in very particular experiences of God among individuals or groups in particular historical settings and . . . the historical context and experience influence the spirituality profoundly.[6]

Spirituality is never neutral, nor is the impact of culture. The contemporary culture, in raising many questions about the meaning of life, is supportive of a search for a viable spirituality. At the same time, other aspects of the culture—such as materialism, the quest for pleasure, and the drvie for success—that claim ultimacy themselves or that deny the basic principles of the gospel are virulent opponents of an authentic spiritual life.

Perhaps the most consistent of characteristics of the present day culture is the rapid acceleration of change in all aspects of life. In our American society we have moved from a post-Depression era to phenomenal economic growth which has resulted in both an affluent middle class and much greater extremes of poverty. The "cultural shift" of the last twenty-five years has included the effects of our involvement in war, the arrival of the Space Age, the escalating threat of nuclear catastrophe and technological, industrial and scientific advances that have raised a whole new set of questions for this generation. Robert Bellah and his associates in their perceptive commentary on our culture, *Habits of the Heart*, point out the significance of the Manager and the Therapist in this society, and highlight the pervasive individualism of Americans.[7] All of these societal factors impinge on the life of the contemporary minister.

The impact of change has also had its effects in the Church which is still, over twenty years after the event, trying to realize the vision of the Second Vatican Council. In attempting to implement the documents of the Council in every phase of Catholic life and teaching, the ministers of the Church are often in tension between those people for whom change is radical betrayal of the past, and those for whom change is not swift nor far-reaching enough. The concern among Christians for deepening roots in the faith is balanced by new awarenesses that result from the expansion of knowledge and rich contributions from many aspects of the culture.

Within the Church itself change has had both positive and problematic effects. The proclamation of the "universal call to holiness" of all the baptized as enunciated by the *Dogmatic Constitution on the Church* of the Council (a. 40) has restored lay persons to their own dignity as Christians, and the *Decree on the Laity* has fostered the movement of laity into all aspects of the Church's life and ministry that are open to the non-ordained. Women and men in religious life have gone through a traumatic period of renewal in which every aspect of their lives has been examined and questioned in the light of the new awareness sparked by the theology, philosophy and psychology of this age. The turmoil that ensued resulted in the loss of many full-time professional ministers, but the re-commitment and renewed dedication to the new demands of ministry of those who remained or who have more recently entered into religious life has been a source of energy and hope. The challenge to laity, clergy and religious to collaborate in new ways for the growth of the Kingdom is an ongoing one and will be even more significant as fewer persons enter religious congregations and diocesan clergy and more lay persons respond to the call to full or part-time ministry.

Many observers believe that the pace of change will not be slowing down. The need to maintain some equilibrium is encumbent upon all who wish to serve in this Church in this period of history. Rahner has pointed out that in the two thousand years of the existence of the Church we have had two main periods, the Jewish Catholic Church of early beginnings and the Roman Catholic Church of all the subsequent centuries. Now, Rahner predicted, we are entering the third great period, that of the World or Universal Church in which the Western culture, which is the dominant influence in our country, is sharing the stage with a variety of world cultures, mainly from the East and the Third World. This shift of influence and of the center of Christianity will continue to affect all in the Church in years to come as the Church itself becomes more truly Catholic. This multi-cultural impact is already being experienced in some ways in many parts of the United States and provides great challenges for spirituality and for ministry.

In this chapter I have described or attempted to clarify concepts which are important background for the chapters which follow. They also indicate the importance of drawing on the tradition in spirituality, while allowing for the influence of the contemporary cultural situation on the experience and activity of the minister.

The following chapters will present key ideas to be explored concerning prayer and action, contemplation and ministerial activity and offer possibilities for integration in the spiritual life of the minister. For each chapter there will be a discussion of what I consider important aspects, based on tradition, insights from the literature and my experience and that of those with whom I have been engaged in ministry. This will be followed by Reflection Activities and Suggested Readings to assist those using this book in personal integration of the material presented. Although there are additional aspects to the question of contemporary spirituality which will need to be addressed by others, I hope that this work will make an important contribution, both by its content and method.

3

Prayer and Action

I would like to introduce this chapter by a story taken from *Tales of a Magic Monastery* by Theophane the Monk.

What Do They Need?

There's a monk there who will never give you advice, but only a question. I was told his questions could be very helpful. I sought him out. "I am a parish priest," I said. "I'm here on retreat. Could you give me a question?"

"Ah, yes," he answered. "My question is, 'What do they need?'"

I came away disappointed. I spent a few hours with the question, writing out answers, but finally I went back to him.

"Excuse me. Perhaps I didn't make myself clear. Your question has been helpful, but I wasn't so much interested in thinking about my apostolate during this retreat. Rather I wanted to think seriously about my own spiritual life. Could you give me a question for my own spiritual life?"

"Ah, I see. Then my question is, 'What do they REALLY need?'"[1]

This story highlighted a familiar tension, perhaps a perennial challenge, to see the relationship between a minister's "spiritual life" and "active life," or, to find the integration that discovers life as a whole. In this chapter I will discuss prayer and action by looking at these elements in the life of Jesus, in the history of our spiritual tradition, and in the lives of those engaged in ministry today.

A. The Experience and Teaching of Jesus

"Rising early the next morning, he went off to a lonely place in the desert; there he was absorbed in prayer." (Mark 1:35)

In the heart of the first chapter of his gospel where Jesus is busy calling his disciples, curing the sick and preaching the good news of the coming of the Kingdom, Mark inserts this statement of contrast—the early, solitary, deep prayer of Jesus. Each of the evangelists present Jesus as a man of both action and prayer. I would like to highlight several aspects in the biblical presentation of Jesus that are important considerations for apostolic persons.

1. The Prayer of Jesus

The most significant aspect of Jesus' prayer is that it was always directed to the Father, to "Abba," the focus and source of Jesus' life, of his mission, of his whole being. Jesus sought intimacy with God in the quiet, solitary times and places in the desert, on the mountain, on the lake, in the garden, in order to allow the Father to minister to him. He is at prayer before his baptism, before beginning his public ministry, before choosing his disciples, before entering Jerusalem for the final days, and on the eve of his death when he struggled in the garden to accept the Father's will and its impending call to kenosis, to self-emptying. Jesus' prayer was one of discernment, of listening to know God's desires in order to fulfill them. "My food is to do the will of him who sent me." (John 4:34) As discerning prayer, it was oriented toward action, toward his mission for the Kingdom. It was also, as Luke states on several occasions, prayer in the Spirit who "led" him (Luke 4:1).

Jesus also prayed with and for others: the widow of Naim, Peter, Lazarus, his executioners, his disciples at the Last Supper, and many whom he healed. He prayed in many different moods—joy, sadness, fear, compassion, gratitude, darkness. As an observant Jew, he prayed at the prescribed times and rituals, and he joined in the prayer of the community in the synagogue and the temple.

Jesus prayed because he was human as well as divine, because prayer was essential to his life and mission. He prayed because he needed clarity, needed to be uniquely open and present to Abba, needed times of calmness and interior focus. He came to prayer to receive the continuing gift of the Father's love, and he prayed for others that they might also experience this love.

2. Jesus' Contemplative Awareness in the Whole of his Life.

The accounts of Jesus' ministry, of his active daily encounter with people, are marked by his awareness of God's continuing presence. At one point he instructs his disciples "about praying always and not losing heart." (Luke 18:1) Through his own example he shows this to be possible through a focused awareness of God in the midst of his busy, at times hectic and pressured days. An indication of this awareness spontaneously bursts forth from his lips when his disciples return to recount the success of their mission and Jesus declares, "I thank you, Father, because what you have hidden from the learned and the clever, you have revealed to merest children." (Luke 10:21)

In each of the stories of Jesus' meeting with individual persons, there is a contemplative openness on Jesus' part to the uniqueness of the other in his or her need or situation. Many examples could be cited: the woman at the well in Sicar, the bent woman, the man at the pool of Bethsaida, the blind Bartimaeus, the leper, the rich young man, Nicodemus, the paralytic, and so many others who came to a new sense of self and wholeness because of this encounter. This open, aware presence to all events is what William Callahan calls "noisy contemplation."[2] This attentive stance toward life, toward the presence and activity of God in each instance, was the ordinary, prayerful posture of Jesus. As Jon Sobrino has so powerfully stated:

> The God of Jesus is a greater God, with a concrete will for his kingdom. Hence Jesus' prayer is a quest for his will and submissiveness to it. That is the concrete way in which he allows himself to be overtaken by God's transcendence. The God of Jesus is also a God of love. Hence the locale of Jesus' prayer is the praxis of love. On the one hand this praxis is a result of the word that Jesus has heard; on the other hand it is the cause of the words that Jesus will enunciate in his own prayer. Hence the locale of Jesus' prayer is not some vague contemplative attitude, nor some vague subjective intention to make contact with God. Instead it is the place where one objectively encounters God by hearing his will and then doing it.[3]

3. Jesus' Teaching

Jesus stressed that the two great commandments were love of God and love of others. In his life and in his teaching he showed how these were not separate but united—a lesson that his followers through the ages have comprehended with difficulty. In various places in the gospels Jesus criticizes inauthentic prayer, that which is self-centered, ostentatious, wordy, hollow or alienating. He condemns those who claim to be perfect observers of ritual prayer and fail to respond to the needs of the poor in their midst, or those who fail to understand their own need of God. (cf. Matt. 6:5-8; 7:21; Lk. 18:11; Mk.12:38,40)

Jesus' prayerfulness drew others to him with the request, "Lord, teach us to pray." The response was to invite his followers into the same attitude toward prayer which was his own, to "Our Father," to praise Abba, to know and do God's will, to be loving and forgiving, and to be preserved from evil. It was the prayer Jesus prayed in the garden, that "not my will but thine be done." The goal of prayer is presented as union with God, a union that is effected through identification with the will and plan of God for God's coming Kingdom.

4. Jesus and the Disciples

In addition to teaching his disciples to pray by example and by word, Jesus also initiated them into the value of time apart from their busy active ministry. In his solicitude for them, he invited them into "quality time" with him, "Come away to a solitary place and rest a while." (Mark 6:31) The ministers needed to be ministered to by the Lord. The burdens of the active apostolate were not to be borne alone. "Come to me all you who labor and I will refresh you . . . ." (Matthew 11:28)

In his Priestly Prayer on the eve of his death (John 17) Jesus prayed to Abba for his disciples that they might be cared for and kept in his Name. They were sent into the world to work for God's reign among his people, yet they needed the powerful protection of God from the evil one and consecration in truth for their mission. It was the love of God in which they lived and which lived in them that would be their strength.

In the conclusion of Matthew's Gospel the Risen Jesus commissions his disciples to "Go . . . baptize . . . teach," or, in other words, to actively minister. Yet the ministry is to be shared. His final promise is that, "I am with you always . . . ." (Matthew 28:20) The challenge for the minister is to be open to Jesus' companioning ministry. How to be open to this Presence? How to experience his Presence in the midst of activity?

B. A Brief Overview of the Issue in the History of the Spiritual Tradition

Stemming from the growth of monasticism in the East, the early tradition of Christian spirituality stressed contemplation as the perfection of the Christian life. Drawing on the philosophical thought of the Greeks, which esteemed the theoretical life over the practical life, the tension between contemplation and action was expressed mainly in looking at these as two different styles of life. Gradually spiritual writers from Origen onward began to discuss contemplation and action as two different stages in the spiritual journey. Action was conceived of as ascetical practice that prepared for contemplation, but contemplation continued to be the ideal, considered the goal and fulfillment of Christian life. Origen introduced the biblical comparison of Martha and Mary as the basis for this evaluation, and his followers down to Pseudo-Dionysius (c. 600 AD) fostered the teaching that all was to be sacrificed for prayer, i.e., contemplative prayer. Action was at times looked on with suspicion, as an obstacle to prayer. Love of God seemed somehow to be divorced from love of neighbor, and the example and teaching of Jesus in this regard lost prominence.

However, among the Fathers of the Church in the West, the pastoral concerns for the Church and the call to the love and service of Jesus Christ and his Kingdom, led to a concern for a life which would combine both prayer and action, a "middle way" in which contemplation and action would complement each other. One such example is the quotation from Gregory the Great:

> One must be well aware that, while a good method of life requires that we pass from the active to the contemplative life, it will however be useful for the soul to come back from the contemplative to the active life so that the flame lit by contemplation may give its perfection to action. Thus, the active life must lead us to contemplation and this, in its turn, under the inspiration of what we have considered interiorly will lead us to action.[4]

In the Western spiritual tradition contemplation and action continued to be seen as a continuum within which persons moved. The question was not either one or the other, but rather, how to hold them together in a creative tension.

In the sixth century, St. Benedict, the founder of Western monasticism, gathered lay men who desired to live the Christian life according to the gospel into community. Benedict's norm has been expressed as prayer and work in community. He does not use the word "contemplation" in his Rule. ". . . the spiritual ideal of the Benedictine Rule is achieved through living of the perfect Christian life in a regular balanced cycle of meditative reading of the sacred scripture interspersed with work and the whole life regulated by the chanting of the Divine Office in choir."[5] Of course, the practice of the meditative reading of scripture, *lectio divina*, often led the monk into the graces of contemplation. The initial Benedictine ideal did not focus on work as apostolic service. Rather, it was work in and for the community in an agricultural, stable form of monastic life. The virtues practiced and nourished in community were charity, humility and obedience. The whole structure and pace of the life aimed at balance, and in all, prayer and work, God was praised.

This initial form of monasticism envisioned by Benedict was expanded and gradually changed when Pope Gregory the Great called on the Benedictines to evangelize England. This great missionary activity necessitated monks becoming priests, with the consequent development of schools, teachers, books and libraries, a far cry from the simple farm life. As Lane points out, "Under the missionary demand of the Church, the spiritual ideal shifts from personal sanctification for the individual to apostolic ministry in the service of the Church."[6]

In the following centuries the Benedictines initiated internal reform movements in order to return to the original inspiration of Benedictine life. The reform at Cluny in the tenth century eliminated external ecclesiastical and political control by creating a federation of monasteries. This reform also placed great emphasis on elaborate liturgical celebrations. In the twelfth century the Cistercian reform sought a return to the simplicity of the primitive Rule of St. Benedict. This brought about a simpler liturgy, emphasis on manual labor, simplicity and poverty of life-style, solitude and prayer. This Cistercian branch of the Benedictine tradition has endured and is viable today.

The next major impact in the tradition of spirituality came in the thirteenth century with the beginning of the mendicant orders founded by Dominic and Francis. This was the period of urbanization in Europe, and new forms of religious life arose to meet the needs of the cities. This type of active monastic life involved a flight from the world and those values that were inimical to following Jesus, yet at the same time it called the friars to an active involvement in the world where their ministry was carried on.

The followers of Dominic were priests and much of their work was in schools and universities. The Divine Office (in a simpler form than in the Benedictine tradition) was the basic form of prayer in common, and private contemplative prayer was encouraged. The Dominican motto: Laudare, Benedicere, Predicare (to praise, to bless, to preach) was lived out both in prayer and in action within the newer style of monastic community living.

Thomas Aquinas, perhaps the best known of the Dominicans after their founder, discussed the relationship of action and contemplation in several places in his writings. For Thomas (as for Jesus), the supreme law is the law of love. Both contemplation and action flow from this one love of God. Thomas viewed contemplation as really superior to action since its goal was divine and it would be our life in eternity. Yet, in this world Thomas viewed the "mixed life," active religious life which had its source in contemplation, as a more perfect way of life than the purely contemplative. His teaching is summed up in the formula *contemplata aliis tradere*, "to hand on what one has contemplated." In this view, contemplation is presupposed, but there is no doubt as to the importance and necessity of action.

Franciscan mendicant friars were at first not priests and their ministry was social and pastoral work in the towns and cities. Authentic spirituality for Francis was composed of a life of religious experience and prayer as well as service. In the Rule of 1221 it is stated that ". . . the servants of God must always give themselves totally to prayer or to some good work." (Chapter VII)[7] The only prescribed common prayer in The Later Rule (1223), Chapter III, is the Divine Office.[8] However a prescription in Chapter V on "The Manner of Working" indicated the pervasive spirit of prayer in all of life.

> Those brothers to whom the Lord has given the grace of working should do their work faithfully and devotedly so that, avoiding idleness, the enemy of the soul, they do not extinguish the Spirit of holy prayer and devotion to which all other things of our earthly existence must contribute.[9]

Francis himself received the graces of mystical prayer and contemplative union with God. This was reflected in his vision of the value of creation and of the dignity of all persons in contrast to the classist prejudices and materialism of his time. "What surfaces most of all from the early sources is a *contemplative outlook* on all of life and creation, whereby Francis was able to see all of reality as a gift of God and render due acknowledgment and praise."[10]

Prayer, fraternity, community and poverty were the consistent ideals of the Franciscan vision and the foundation for a very active and public ministry. However, during his lifetime, Francis allowed for those drawn to a more contemplative life-style through his "Rule for Hermitages." Later, in the sixteenth century, the Capuchin branch of the Order would be established as a more contemplative group following the Franciscan charism.

The apostolic monastic form of life combining prayer and ministry begun by the mendicants was a major religious force in the medieval Church. Alongside of it there also began to flourish a renewed interest in the "cult of contemplation" with the Rhineland mystics, Meister Eckhart and his disciples, and the English mystics, Richard Rolle, Julian of Norwich and Walter Hilton in the fourteenth century. The Spanish mystics of the sixteenth century, particularly Teresa of Avila and John of the Cross, further developed this contemplative tradition.

The reform movement unleashed in the Church in the sixteenth century was the impetus for many innovations and much fervor and excitement in ministry. The spirit of the age was caught and exemplified in the charismatic person of Ignatius Loyola. At a time when holiness was linked to contemplation, Ignatius, conscious of the great needs of the reform of the Church, was led to develop a spirituality for active service. It was the "particular grace of St. Ignatius to recall that the spiritual life is not first of all a problem of prayer or a problem of activity, but a fidelity to God which demands fidelity to divine tasks."[11] Ignatius' own conversion experience was a total "falling-in-love with God," as Lonergan would define it. This love had as its focus the service of God through prayer and activity which would assist in the growth of the Kingdom of God. The mystical vision of Ignatius expressed in the *Spiritual Exercises* was one in which God was to be sought and found "in all things." Contrary to many of his contemporaries, Ignatius viewed the world as the arena of God's activity. Where the earlier Benedictine spiritualities had emphasized the transcendence of God experienced in liturgy, lectio and contemplation, Ignatius saw also the immanence of God, present and working in the world. Union with God in his view, was not only a union in prayer, but a union of will with God in the midst of activity. The work of the apostolate then, instead of being an obstacle to union with God, may be the privileged place of this union.

Ignatius himself enjoyed the mystical graces of deep prayer and experience of God's presence, but he used the term "prayer" at times to designate both "a particular and definite exercise" and also "continuous union with God in activity."[12] In the description of Ignatius' spirituality given by Jerome Nadal, "in all things, actions, conversations, he felt and contemplated the presence of God and the attraction of spiritual things. He was a contemplative in action, something he expressed habitually in the words: 'we must find God in all things'."[13]

This was the spiritual challenge offered to his followers. It was the vision embodied in the *Spiritual Exercises,* especially in the Principle and Foundation, the Contemplation for Attaining Divine Love, and the Rules for the Discernment of Spirits. The latter are especially important for those desiring to serve God by conformity to God's Will and cooperation with God, working with God for his Kingdom. As Harvey Egan has stressed:

> Not only mystical prayer unites a person to God. For Ignatius, self-emptying service for God's honor alone and forgetting oneself for the sake of others are also significant means of uniting a person with God.[14]

Ignatius refused to prescribe the Divine Office in common for his Society, thus breaking a tradition of communal prayer in religious congregations from the time of Benedict. In fidelity to their fourth vow, Jesuits were to be free for mission, to go even alone or in twos wherever needed, "to go anywhere in the world." The obligation of regular hours of prayer in common might prevent their availability for the work of the apostolate, for missionary activity.

In Chapter 5, we will explore some implications of Ignatius' insights. In this section, the significance of his contribution to the evolution of apostolic religious life must be emphasized.

The trend toward the more active involvement of religious continued from this period on. Vincent de Paul in the seventeenth century when describing the movement from prayer to ministry spoke of "Leaving God for God." Louise de Marillac, who shared his vision, became the foundress of the "Daughters of Charity" rather than use the term "religious" in order that they would be free to serve the poor and not be bound by cloister. This also was the original inspiration of Francis de Sales and Jane de Chantal in the foundation of the Visitation. However, their prescription for the sisters to regularly visit the ill and the poor in their homes was ultimately removed from the Rule at the insistence of ecclesiastical authorities, who refused to allow religious women not bound by cloister into their dioceses. The apostolic life for women had a much more difficult struggle to survive in the Church than that for men.

The nineteenth century saw the great outburst of active ministry as religious women and men responded to the tremendous social, moral, and religious needs of people in Europe, in Asia and in America. However the chief models for religious life, especially for women, were monastic, with cloister, choir, prayer and community as strong determining factors. The tension of work and prayer at times was quite unbalanced, and often the vision of founders and foundresses for more apostolic involvement was thwarted by ecclesiastical structures.

C. The Question Today

There is a great amount of support for the insight that people are hungering for prayer and for assistance in their spiritual lives. This priority ought to be addressed by those in ministry. However, it is the underlying thesis of this book that ministers need to grow in these areas themselves in order to live fuller and more integrated lives. Some of the issues for ministers today are outlined here.

1. Past experience of the ministers—Most of the active religious and even the secular clergy have been formed in a model of spirituality that continued the monastic style and rhythm. Consequently, they have been juggling the questions and tensions of time for prayer, lack of interest or lack of growth in prayer, and the demands of very active ministries. For some the outcome has been guilt, for others a moving toward one extreme or the other, often more toward activism.

The lay persons involved in ministry have had varying degrees of ministerial formation. Those who have been prepared well have more usually been able to acquire intellectual, managerial and interpersonal skill training, but rarely have experienced spiritual formation.

2. Attitudes—Ministers have inherited many of the attitudes and ideas from the past which were discussed in the history of the tradition. Relevant to our topic is the idea that prayer is more important or "higher" than activity, that action, while necessary, is inferior. Most contemporary Christians were also not encouraged to practice contemplative forms of prayer, nor to expect the graces of deeper prayer.

In addition, biases from the contemporary culture are subtle influences, such as those which question counter-cultural values like solitude and silence, or the non-compulsive, non-productive, waiting attitude necessary for contemplation. ". . . non-achievement time will appear a waste and avoided. Time for prayer will lose its value because I am not *doing* anything, not helping anyone."[15]

3. Personal Growth—Ministers are not very different from other adult Christians. They are on various levels of maturity in many aspects of their development: psychological, religious, spiritual, moral. Many have been wounded in their life experiences, and how they have dealt with this will help or hinder their capacity to minister. Thus, processes for reflecting on life experiences and aids in noticing invitations to grow are important components of a program of formation for ministry.

Motivation for entering into ministry can also be varied. In addition to those with a sound awareness of a vocation to serve, there are also those motivated by intense activism, which at times can seem to be a distraction from other aspects of life. The contemporary phenomenon of burnout is especially a problem for many in ministry, where personal needs and values can impel ministers to over-work, losing spiritual dynamism for their activity. These and other areas of personal growth offer a challenge both to the ministers themselves and those charged with their ongoing formation.

4. Formation—These are only a few of the considerations related to the question of a spirituality for ministry today which need to be addressed. The goal of adult maturity is a basic one. It can be encouraged and assisted by helping ministers grow in self-awareness, in reflection on experience, in making connections between their own story and the stories of Scripture, of tradition and of the contemporary world. Attention to the ongoing invitation to personal conversion is crucial. Subsequent chapters will focus on three main areas of importance in the process of spiritual formation: Prayer, action and integration.

D. Reflection Activities

(These may be led by a facilitator or done alone. It is important that some writing be done after each reflection, and when possible some small or large group sharing to assist in processing the experience.)

1. Take some time to reflect on your life story as your personal salvation history. You might do it in stages, noting at each stage who God was for you, to whom you prayed, the persons who made God real for you, the key events, the patterns of how God dealt with you, the ups and downs of the journey. You might use a scripture passage to help you enter into this reflection prayerfully (e.g. Deuteronomy 1:29-33; Psalm 139, Luke 24:13-35). Let God tell you how God was present on your journey. At the end, spend some time with these questions: Who is God for you now? Who are you for God? Where are you on your journey with God?

2. Reflect on the wholeness of your faith experience that has brought you to today. What do you really believe? "Know" in your heart? What gives meaning to your life? What has energized you? What is it that you want to share with others?

3. Ask Jesus to allow you to be with him in his prayer to the Father. Some places in Scripture that may assist your prayer are: Matthew 6:6-13, Luke 3:21-22, Luke 9:28-36, Mark 1:35, Luke 6:12-13. Be present to the scene, enter into the prayer. Pray as you are moved to pray.

4. How have you been able to balance prayer and action in your life? Where have you experienced tension? Has the tradition in which you were formed assisted or hindered you in this?

E. Suggested Readings

1. *The Prayer of Jesus*

a. William Callahan, S.J., in *Contemporary Spirituality: Responding to the Divine Initiative* (ed. Francis Eigo, OSA) Villanova, Pa.: Villanova University Press, 1983.

b. Segundo Galilea, *Following Jesus.* Maryknoll, N.Y.: Orbis Books, 1981.

c. Jon Sobrino, Chapter 5 "The Prayer of Jesus," in *Christology at the Crossroads.* Maryknoll, N.Y.: Orbis Books, 1978.

2. *The Spiritual Tradition*

a. Thomas M. Gannon and George W. Traub, *The Desert and the City.* Chicago: Loyola University Press, 1984.

b. George Lane, S.J., *Christian Spirituality,* Chicago: Loyola University Press, 1984.

c. John Lozano, et al., *Ministerial Spirituality and Religious Life.* Religious Life Series. Chicago: Claret Center for Resources in Spirituality, 1986.

4

Prayer and Contemplation

Previous chapters have described discipleship as a response to an invitation to intimacy with Jesus, and have quoted Lonergan's description of religious faith as falling-in-love with God. These insights speak to the obvious need for a deep relationship through personal prayer, for time to be present to and to be with God, while also leading a life of active service in ministry for the Kingdom. My experience in spiritual direction and retreat work, which is also shared by many of my colleagues, indicates that growth in personal prayer is an area calling for great attention in the spiritual lives of ministers. The prevalence of burnout in ministry and the persons who confess to being "eaten up" by their work are further evidence of this lack of an integrated spirituality.

This chapter sketches an approach to formation in prayer for ministers, leading to a focus on contemplative prayer and a contemplative attitude. It will of necessity be done in broad strokes, leading the facilitator or instructor to expand where needed. It concludes with some reflective activities and forms of prayer to encourage personal involvement and experience, and also some resources for further consultation.

A. Key Concepts Concerning Prayer

In beginning to develop attitudes about prayer and to help others explore new ways of prayer it is important to address some possible misconceptions. Recently, in a short article I addressed some of the paradoxes or seeming contradictions involved in approaching prayer.[1] These flow from my conviction that prayer is primarily our response to the Presence of God as God reveals himself to us.[2] The first paradox stems from the truth that prayer is a gift. The desire to pray is in itself an invitation from God who wants the relationship with us to grow. We cannot deserve or earn this gift, yet there must be something we can do on our part of the relationship. The one thing we can do is to open ourselves to receive this gift of prayer, and this openness presupposes many things. It means a desire for the gift, a receptive attitude, and an effort to let go of whatever blocks the possibility of receiving the fullness of God's Presence in our life. Since the gift God gives in prayer is actually God himself, whatever assists attentive waiting and listening is important.

A second paradox is our use of phrases like "seeking God," "searching for God," or "wanting to enter the Presence of God," when describing our initial activity in prayer. The reality is that God is always present. As Paul reminded the people of Athens, ". . . he is not far from any one of us. In him we live and move and have our being." (Acts 17:27-28) Instead of our searching for God then, prayer is rather allowing ourselves to be found by God. As Abraham Heschel has written, "We approach him not by making him the object of our thinking, but by discovering ourselves as the objects of his thinking."[3] Prayer is coming home to ourselves and discovering God in the depths of our own heart.

Another paradox involves the mystery of the relationship between God and ourselves. Perhaps if we become better, more loving, etc. we will experience God's love more? Or should we pray more in order to become more loving? Here the focus is on what *we* do, rather than on God. The great mystery is that God loves us now just as we are, not because we are good but because God is good, and God's goodness overflows in his love. If prayer were time to allow God to love us, to grow in awareness of God's love, then loving in return would resolve itself as God's love became the source of ours.

There are other aspects of prayer that challenge our usual view of reality. Contrary to most kinds of growth, growth in prayer is growth in simplicity rather than in complexity. As we come closer to God, or allow God to approach us, prayer requires fewer if any words, less thought or activity on our part. The goal is to be filled by God, and so the desire should be to allow ourselves to become empty enough to receive, to let go of controlling "my" prayer, so that the Lord can lead. We need to become more quiet and content with waiting, in order that the power and love of God can work in the hidden places of our being, while it may seem that "nothing is going on."

While prayer is one of the most personal activities of our lives, unique though it may be, our prayer is not only ours. As Paul states often, our life is life in Christ, and our prayer is always with Jesus and in Jesus. He lives to intercede for us to God, as the author of the Letter to the Hebrews has told us. (Heb. 7:25) In Romans 8:26-27, Paul reminds us that ". . . when we cannot choose words in order to pray properly, the Spirit himself expresses our plea . . ." Our prayer is always somehow Trinitarian, caught up in the activity of God within us, leading us to a transformation that is beyond our dreams or comprehension.

Thomas Merton has summed up much of what I believe is important about prayer:

> In prayer we discover what we already have. You start where you are and you deepen what you already have, and you realize that you are already there. We already have everything, but we don't know it and we don't experience it. Everything has been given to us in Christ. All we need is to experience what we already possess.[4]

B. Aids for Prayer

We learn to pray by praying, and the prime teacher of prayer is the Holy Spirit. Yet there are things we can do to open ourselves more fully to God's Presence. In forming ministers to a life of prayer these are some of the areas that need to be emphasized:

1. Silence—an appreciation and experience of silence in order to be able to listen to God and to notice the movements in the depths of one's heart. (The heart is the place of prayer.)

2. Solitude—seeking and accepting time alone, in order to be present to God. Alfred North Whitehead has defined religion as what one does with solitude. Many people's prayer benefits from encouragement toward solitude and creative ways to focus during time alone.

3. Discipline—referring to those exercises of discipleship that enable one to be really present to God in order to listen. (cf. Isaiah 50:4 "Each morning he wakes me to hear, to listen like a disciple.") Some aspects of discipline would be the actual decision for a life of prayer, the time, place and posture conducive to prayer. Whatever would lessen bodily tension

and help one to be still and present should be explored. Anthony de Mello has suggested that the greatest obstacle to prayer is tension.

4. Awareness—the only time we ever encounter God is in the present moment, yet it is extremely difficult for many persons to be really present. De Mello has developed a number of exercises drawn from the tradition of the East that have been very helpful for myself and for many to whom I have given instruction in prayer. These assist in moving from the head to the heart by heightening awareness, expanding the experience of oneself, dissipating tension and allowing the Lord to move and touch a person more deeply. They aid in paying attention to both external and internal reality. Some exercises from *Sadhana*[5] are outlined at the conclusion of this chapter.

C. Variety of Approaches to Prayer

I have encountered many ministers who are "stuck" in prayer or who have given up what seemed to be meaningful prayer, and one of the most common explanations for this is that they never were encouraged to change their form of personal prayer, or they lacked even the initiative to look for more creative ways to pray. A prime source for prayer, and rightly so, has been Scripture, the privileged focus for encounter with God's Word, yet even here, the wealth of possibilities in the tradition has been overlooked. Pedro Arrupe, S.J., in writing to the Jesuits stressed the importance of Scripture for contemporary spirituality:

> To live today, at every moment and in every mission, the life of a "contemplative in action" supposes a gift and a pedagogy of prayer that will give us the capacity for a renewed "reading" of reality (all of reality) from the point of view of the Gospel and for continual confrontation of that reality with the Gospel.[6]

When we pray with Scripture we are entering into the same model of reflection of the Whiteheads described in the first chapter. The biblical tradition, viewed through the lens of the contemporary cultural milieu, is brought into engagement with the praying person's own experience. The stories of the tradition touch the unique personal story and shed light on that story for living today. St. Bernard has suggested that "we must drink from our own wells." Ministers should drink from the wellsprings of Scripture often and be helped also to recognize the wellsprings within their own experience.

There are many resources for developing prayer with Scripture, some of which I will suggest later. All can be located somewhere in the schema describing the prayer of the early monks, which has been transmitted in different ways through the history of spirituality: *Lectio Divina, Meditatio, Oratio, Contemplatio*. (Thomas Keating has given an excellent history of this development in *Open Mind, Open Heart.*[7])

In a spiritual formation program, I would strongly urge actual prayer experiences in the group setting, led by the facilitator, with some previous explanation, time for quieting and focusing, the actual prayer time, and time for reflection on the prayer afterwards, which could also include journaling. Common sharing after would also be beneficial, and could become a form of group spiritual direction. Forms of prayer to be shared in this way are:

- *Lectio Divina*
- "Ignatian" Contemplation on a passage
- Praying with a symbol from Scripture—e.g., water, seed, shepherd, bread, etc.
- Praying with a question from Scripture—e.g., "Who do you say I am?"; "What do you want me to do for you?"
- Use of imagination with Scripture as a starting place and leading a guided imagery meditation.

These and other types of scriptural prayer can assist ministers to encounter God or Jesus in their prayer and gradually to grow in deeper understanding of who God is for them and who they are for God. The ministry, which is an expression of their relationship with God and the desire to be involved with Jesus in his work of the Kingdom, will take on a new dimension. Too much of prayer in the past for many has centered solely on meditation as an intellectual or reflective activity, with little attention to affectivity, imagery, dialogue, or more contemplative prayer. Head-centered prayer often did not allow God to move the prayer deeply, nor to let control of the prayer be more God's leading than the person's. De Mello points out that the head isn't a bad place to begin prayer, but it shouldn't just remain a head activity. Moving to the heart enables a more spontaneous and real encounter with God.

D. Contemplation

Karl Rahner has stated his belief that ". . . the devout Christian of the future will either be a mystic, that is one who has experienced something, or he will cease to be any-thing at all."[8] I would add, "experienced Someone," since it is important that a relationship with God be real and interpersonal, not only notional. If Rahner's claim is true for the Christian, how much more true ought it to be for the Christian minister, whose whole life activity should be centered in a loving relationship with God. To persevere and grow in living the Christian mystery in a time when Christianity may be less acceptable and more countercultural in society, requires a depth of prayer and a clarity of perception that can only be termed mystical. There are many modes of mystical prayer and in speaking of a spiritual formation for ministry, I am concerned with how to encourage and support an "ordinary mysticism" and contemplative prayer. It is a matter of preparation and affirming a direction, aware that God can lead and move a person in a much deeper relationship once the desire and openness are present.

In the monastic schema of prayer as found, for example, in Pachomius and Guido, the *lectio divina, meditatio,* and *oratio* culminated in *contemplatio.* Contemplation was seen as the normal development of a life of prayer. The movement in prayer from thoughts, words, symbols or images that mediate God's Presence into a quieter mode of prayer and awareness of being with God is a response to God's invitation and attraction. It is God's desire for intimacy with us, expressed in numerous ways in Scripture, that is the source of this call to a more contemplative prayer.

To the praying person, it is an invitation to enter into the stillness of one's own heart, to listen, to be open, to be formed by God who is working deep within. In Lonergan's imperative, it is to "Be attentive," which aids in clarifying the vision that inspires and informs all our activity. It was Simone Weil's insight that "absolute attention is prayer."

Contemplative prayer involves an openness to the mystery of God, a focus on the Other, who gifts us with Presence. It demands an *active* listening, a listening heart. It is a way of being, not something we possess. Contemplation requires a degree of maturity, and is the result of preparation, of time, and of growth—which is ultimately the Lord's gift, which must be desired and accepted. A vital attitude of contemplation is receptivity, an openness to receive, which flows from the awareness of one's own emptiness. True self-knowledge, which realizes our own weakness and limitation, creates the "space" for God, who enriches us precisely in our poverty.

Contemplative prayer is more a matter of the heart than of the head. It is intuitive knowing of the Other which comes from loving. It involves sensitivity to inner movements, awareness of feelings and affectivity. Love is the motive for contemplation, but it is not a love that merely rests in the enjoyment of the Beloved. Contemplation involves commitment of the whole of oneself to this loving God, and concern for all that God loves.

The effects of contemplation involve a transformation of the praying, loving person. In Leonardo Boff's terminology, the effect is transparency: the divine is revealed in the human, the human is realized in the divine. The "inner eye" is opened, the eye of love, which reveals one's solidarity with all others and issues a call to a universal love.

In the tradition of Christian spirituality there are two prominent forms of contemplation which seem quite diverse, yet both of which lead to a deeper awareness and union with God. It is important to distinguish between these, both for those who are in initial stages of growth, and also by way of confirmation and support for those who may be more experienced in prayer.

1. *Kataphatic contemplation*—stresses the affirmation of God's Presence in all of creation, the fullness of awareness and perception which is typified in the Ignatian charism of "finding God in all things." Called at times the "via positiva," it has a very incarnational basis, and at times, what today might be called a creation-centered spirituality foundation.

2. *Apophatic contemplation*—is an experience of negation or at times, apparent absence of God. It is characterized by darkness, nothingness, detachment, unknowing, the Cross. Called "via negativa," it is described in the teaching of Pseudo-Dionysius, in the fourteenth century classic work, *The Cloud of Unknowing,* and in the writings of John of the Cross, who speaks of the two dark nights, of the spirit and of the soul.

A facilitator or instructor in a spiritual formation program is not so much called to teach contemplation as to lead others into the quiet of their own hearts where God can teach and form them. However, it is important to be able to be a guide on the way, to be knowledgeable enough to support, affirm, confirm and challenge when appropriate. The books of several authors listed as resources in this chapter or in the Bibliography are very rich sources, e.g. the works of Green, Merton, Keating and Shannon.

This is a brief outline of the process of contemplative prayer that might be helpful for understanding:

1. Quieting of body, mind, faculties (memory, imagination, understanding less active).

2. Development of heart—lowered mental activity allows for increased psychic energy at deeper levels. Greater awareness, intensity, expansion of consciousness; affective, loving, simple response.

3. Focused awareness—attention, open waiting, active stretching out to God, passive resting in God, quiet alertness.

4. Wordless communication—faculty of the will is active in faith and love.

5. Letting-go—surrender, emptying, kenosis; poverty of spirit; letting God mold, as a potter forms clay. Darkness, purification, stripping; acceptance of the darkness.

6. Transformation—communion with God. Willingness to be changed by this relationship beyond that which occurs in all significant relationships. Re-created through encounter with God, with the Risen Jesus, with the Spirit.

7. Effects—increased self-knowledge and acceptance; fruits of the Spirit (cf. Galatians 5:20): love, joy, peace, inner freedom, integration, solidarity with others.

One form of contemplative prayer which dates back to the earliest monastic traditions and which has gained great acceptance today is Centering Prayer. It involves internal repetition of a short mantra-like prayer which brings the pray-er to the center of his/her being. The work of Dom John Main, O.S.B. in Canada and that of the American Trappists, Keating, Pennington and Menninger, have made this simple form of prayer accessible to people in every kind of living and working situation. The simplicity of method and the gradually perceived effects of Centering Prayer encourage a more contemplative approach and a basic, comfortable structure for prayer. It is recommended that this prayer be prayed for twenty to thirty minutes twice a day. An outline for Centering Prayer to be followed alone or with a group is presented in the suggested activities at the conclusion of this chapter.

The Directory for the Jesus Caritas Priests' Fraternity invites members to reflect on the question, "In the midst of all that I am doing for Christ, what is Christ doing within me?" Growth in contemplative prayer allows the deeper listening and awareness implied in this question, as well as the freeing, open stance which facilitates God's action within. Contemplation thus supports a resolution of the underlying tension addressed in this book, which for ministers is sometimes posed as: Where is the emphasis—on being or doing? Growth in union with God on ever deeper levels promotes a unity within oneself, so that who I am and what I do are not separate but one.

E. Contemplative Attitude

Contemplative prayer promotes and is also assisted by a contemplative attitude toward life. In Chapter 3 we noted Jesus' contemplative awareness in the whole of his life, his attentive stance toward the presence of God in everyday occurrences. Underlying this faith-stance, is the human capacity to be contemplative. We are born with this ability as human persons, but frequently it has been almost "educated out of us" by the emphasis on the rational approach to reality which has predominated in our culture. Contemporary studies on "left brain" and "right brain" activities are contributing toward a new awareness of the need to foster "right brain" utilization and awareness and thus to nurture aspects that can permit the contemplative dimension to develop.

I would like to outline some elements of a contemplative attitude which underlie this important aspect of integrating prayer and ministry.

A contemplative attitude is a stance toward life, a way of experiencing reality which includes:

- Awareness and a savoring of reality
- Appreciation of what is (cp. the poet's appreciation of nature), as opposed to approaching reality with pre-conceived ideas or illusions
- Openness to mystery, awe, surprise, wonder
- Attention, focused *in* the present moment
- Patience, waiting, receptivity

- Listening, noticing, sensitivity
- Gratitude for what is gift
- Affective presence
- A leisurely attitude toward time
- Non-controlling, non-compulsive
- Not "driven," not performance- or production-oriented
- Non-possessive

This stance implies a quality of presence *to* what is, and the capacity to be affected *by* the presence of whatever is. It thus allows God to reveal himself, what God is doing, how God is present in the moment, the person, the event. Henri Nouwen has pointed out that we have to come to recognize God in our own hearts before we can recognize God in the marketplace. The recognition does not imply putting God there, but as Ignatius taught, discovering that God is already there.

Many elements in our culture militate against this contemplative attitude. We experience a narcotizing of awareness, a numbing and blunting of perception, due to intense sense-bombardment. We learn to filter out what isn't meaningful or cannot be handled, but we restrict our awareness and are often scattered and unfocused. Our own radical sinfulness at times also contributes to a lack of focus, when we are motivated by our unfreedoms, restlessness, or boredom. Our cultural drive for production, possession and achievement influence us more than we know. Growth in contemplative awareness is a very countercultural stance.

George Aschenbrenner, S.J., has described the "prayer of the active apostle" as a "distinctly prayerful presence in and through all activity."[9] The effects of growing in this attitude and way of "seeing" reality, together with the attention and focusing of contemplative prayer, lead to greater openness and deeper experience both of oneself and of God. Contemplation supports our ongoing personal conversion, expands our self-knowledge and the acceptance of ourselves, of our weaknesses, sinfulness and limitation because it leads us to poverty of spirit, to a radical dependence on God. It is in prayer that we can struggle with our own darkness and often also, the darkness of our world; and it is in contemplative prayer that we can experience transformation and be enabled to grow toward self-transcendence in love for God and others. Prayer will inform our activity with increased clarity and awareness, help us to be more in the present, and more responsive than reactive. We can grow in inner freedom and peacefulness and be a revealing Presence of God wherever we are.

F. Reflection Activities

1. Time for Reflection

Take some time to become quiet. Then recall some time in your life when you were very aware of God's Presence. Let the occasion come to the forefront of your consciousness. It may be a time that you experienced some natural beauty, it may have been an awareness of God in another person, perhaps a time of prayer or on retreat, or a time when you were surprised by the Lord.

Allow your memory to bring to consciousness as many of the details of the experience as possible. Be there again, see, hear, feel as much as you can. See if you can recapture the spiritual experience you had in the past and bring with you into the present some of the awareness and power that experience was for you.

This is more than thinking about the experience. Be there. Be aware. Notice; feel. At the end of the time, reflect on these questions.

1. What did I know about God at the time? Who was God for me?

2. How did I feel?

3. What did the experience tell me about myself?

4. What does this experience have to say to me now?

2. A Suggested Form for Prayer

Try to use this prayer time as an opportunity to become aware of the Lord's Presence, to reflect, but mainly to listen, to wait for God. There is no amount of thinking to be done, no material "to be covered." Just let God lead you where God wants you to go, to meet you where God wants to encounter you. The goal is to become more aware of God's Presence in your life, of God's love for you, and to respond to that Presence and that love.

Some helpful preliminaries:

1. Settle yourself in a quiet place where you can pray uninhibitedly.

2. Take a posture in which your back is straight but comfortable and that you can maintain for the duration of your prayer.

3. Quiet yourself by some means that you find helpful; e.g., pay attention to your breathing; notice your senses; try to "come home to yourself."

4. Ask the Lord to reveal his Presence to you; become aware of God's nearness and of God's Presence within you. Respond to that Presence.

5. Ask God for whatever grace you feel you would like at this time, or ask God to let you know what gifts God wishes to give you in this prayer.

6. If you are going to use a passage of Scripture for focus in the time for prayer, recall that it is the Lord's own Word to you. Listen quietly and deeply with your inner ear, your heart, to the Word of Scripture, and respond to that Word as you feel drawn to do. There is no quantity of material to be read, just proceed very slowly and stop wherever you meet the Lord or feel God is speaking especially to you at this time. Let the Lord show you; let God tell you!

7. When the time comes to end your prayer, sum up your feelings and your love in your own words to the Lord.

8. Spend a few minutes after your prayer reflecting on the time of prayer: How did it go? Where did I meet the Lord? Were there any words or phrases of Scripture that were especially fruitful? What is going on in your relationship with God? Where does God seem to be leading you? What would you like to happen in your prayer life? What do you think the Lord would like to happen?

3. Exercises for Awareness:

a. De Mello (*Sadhana*) Exercises 1,2,3,5,6,7,11 pp. 1 - 45

b. Edwards (*Living in the Presence*) Exercises 4,5 pp. 36 - 40; Exercise 10 pp. 63 - 64

4. *Lectio Divina:*

a. De Mello Exercise 33, pp. 101 - 105

b. Edwards Exercise 20, pp. 93 - 94

c. Personal and Group *lectio*:

1. Quiet yourself before the Lord, making a simple act of faith, thanksgiving and praise . . . centering for a few moments.

2. Read the Scripture passage slowly (if in a group read aloud.)

3. Again become quiet . . . A certain line, phrase, word may catch your attention . . . Stay with it, repeating slowly as a mantra . . . letting it become quietly a part of your being (if group prayer share your phrase aloud . . . not over and over but once).

4. Read the Scripture passage again slowly (in group read aloud).

5. Again become quiet . . . address God in prayer concerning the word you have received . . . and then listen (if in group, share your prayer when and if you feel called to).

6. Read the Scripture passage again slowly (in group read aloud).

7. Personal *lectio divina* . . . You might continue centering on your mantra or prayer word, reflect on insights, journal your thoughts regarding the word. How does this word touch your life at this particular time? End with the "Our Father."

5. Imaginative Contemplation

a. De Mello Exercise 22, pp. 73 - 79

b. Edwards Exercise 21, pp. 94 - 96

c. Anne Long (*Can Spirituality Be Taught?*) pp. 115 - 120

6. A Centering Prayer Experience

a. Edwards Exercise 5, pp. 40 - 43

b. Trappist Formulation:

Sit comfortably in a chair that will give your back support, and gently close your eyes. It is good to choose a place where you will not be disturbed by any sudden intrusion. A quiet place is helpful, though not essential. 1. Sit relaxed and quiet. 2. Be in faith and love to God who dwells in the center of your being. 3. Take up a love word and let it be gently present, supporting your being to God in faith-filled love. 4. Whenever you become aware of anything else, simply, gently return to the Lord with the use of your prayer word.   5. At the end of your prayer, let the Our Father (or some other prayer) pray itself.

7. Video Reflection

View some of the segments of Anthony de Mello's video presentations and follow the viewing with reflection and discussion. Guides accompany these videos:

A Way to God for Today (Six 30 minute segments)

Wake Up! Spirituality for Today (Three 30 minute segments)

G.   Suggested Readings

1. Anthony de Mello, S.J., *Sadhana: A Way to God.* St. Louis: The Institute of Jesuit Studies, 1978.

2. Tilden Edwards, *Living in the Presence.* San Francisco: Harper & Row, 1987.

3. Thelma Hall, r.c., *Too Deep For Words:* Re-discovering *Lectio Divina.* Mahwah, N.J.: Paulist, 1988.

4. Thomas Kane, "Inhabiting the Gospel," in *Desert Call,* (13/2) Spring 1978.

5. Thomas Keating, *Open Mind, Open Heart.* New York: Amity House, 1986.

6. Anne Long, "What Works?," in *Can Spirituality Be Taught?* (ed. Robson, Jill and Lonsdale, David. London: Association of Centres of Adult Theological Association and British Council of Churches, 1988).

7. Henri Nouwen, *The Way of the Heart.* New York: The Seabury Press, 1981.

8. William H. Shannon, *Seeking the Face of God.* New York: Crossroad, 1988.

9. Carolyn Stahl, *Opening to God.* Nashville, Tenn.: The Upper Room, 1977.

5

Action and Ministry

A. Contemporary Insights Concerning Human Action

After exploring prayer and contemplation as essential components of a real, loving relationship with God, and highlighting the cultivation of a contemplative attitude as openness to the graced dimension of all reality, I would like to focus now on the other half of the dyad being examined in this book, specifically on action.

Insights from our contemporary American culture, especially recent studies in anthropology, have opened up a whole new vista in examining the question of contemplation and action. These insights offer a significant contribution in the process of spiritual formation for ministry.

In the fourth chapter of his book, *Playing in the Gospel*, Thomas Clarke, S.J. suggests that a more contemporary approach to the discussion would be to *begin* with a focus on action. He points out that in all the previous models of spirituality the starting point, the energizing center, was prayer. "The primary encounter with God was conceived to take place in times and spaces apart . . . the flow of spiritual energy was unidirectional, from contemplation to action."[1] Not much attention was paid to the apostolic encounter with God, nor to its effect on prayer.

Following the philosophy and theology of Karl Rahner, Clarke views prayer in its basic sense as identical with faith as a dimension of graced consciousness. Rahner's emphasis on the transcendent dimension in human behavior leads to the insight that each person is in every instance of truly human behavior "being addressed by God in a self-revelation and self-gift that is mediated through some human value."[2] When recognized by faith, this gift asks a response from the person so addressed. This consciousness is the root of radical prayer, when what I *do* is an exercise of faith. In this perspective, both "prayer" and "action" are action.

Influenced by the philosophy of Maurice Blondel, Thomas Clarke describes the components of genuine human action as:

1. Awareness—the contemplative dimension; action is not illusory or addictive action, but is based on receptive openness to what is true and real in the human and the divine. When I act humanly, I am really aware of what I am doing.

2. Freedom—the responsive dimension—action chosen as a "yes" to values, to God, freely willed. When I act humanly, I do what I really want to do. This freedom does not come easily, and so Clarke points out that genuine human action will bear the mark of the Cross. There will be conflict and conquest on the path to liberation when the darkness caused by human sinfulness will eventually be overcome.[3]

Whenever faith/prayer is exercised in this two-fold process of awareness and freedom, the contemplative and responsive dimensions of action are present. Real human action is contemplative action *and* responsive action, freely chosen in awareness. *Thus, all action is contemplative to the degree that it is genuine human action. All contemplation is a form of action provided and to the degree it is truly contemplative.* We do need times for contemplative prayer, to open ourselves to God's action within us, to develop the habit of contemplative/responsive action, as a sign of the seriousness of our search for God, and of our yearning for union with God in freedom. But we also, in Father Clarke's words, often "miss the strength and vitality that can come from meeting God in the very exercise of ministry and all our activities . . . we waste other opportunities for God to renew our strength."[4]

In the September 1987 issue of *Studies in the Spirituality of Jesuits*, Roger Haight also addresses what he calls the "necessary and inner tension between prayer and action."[5] He recalls the words of Ignatius in the *Spiritual Exercises* (#230): "That love ought to manifest itself in deeds rather than in words," as the retreatant reflects on God's deeds of love and is moved to respond in personal surrender and commitment. As one approach to re-interpreting spirituality, Haight develops an anthropology of action based on Maurice Blondel's philosophy in *L'Action*. I would like to outline briefly some of Haight's points that are especially helpful for this discussion, while acknowledging that this summary does not do justice to the depth of his work.

1. Human beings are centers of action and any given person is what he or she does. Action is the name of our existence as well as what we do. Human action is free. We constitute ourselves by our action.

2. The freedom that constitutes action is creative. Human action has eternal value through God's power of creation. Therefore, we have a responsibility for creative action in the world. (cf. Lonergan's imperative, "Be responsible.")

3. Human action interacts with the world and fashions society. Action holds society together.

4. Through God's grace, human action can participate in God's action in the world. God's infinite power grounds and sustains action.

5. Through intentionality, human action based on reflective awareness can reach out toward the ultimate good or Being itself.

6. Decision and action that cooperate with God's intention and action in the world bind a person in a symbiotic and possessive relationship with God.

7. In a spirituality of action two levels interact:
   a. the reflective level—which is one's vision of God and reality
   b. the existential level—comprising the conscious decisions and actions that make persons who they are.

One lives out of a vision of faith. Prayer and contemplation nurture this vision. The *goal* is union with God through action which cooperates with God's action in and for the world.

These summarized insights of Haight's expand our ideas about human action and have many implications for a spirituality of ministry. I hear in them an echo of a statement of John Paul II, "Work in a specific way forms the human person, and in a certain sense creates him or her." What is designated is not just *doing* or mere performance, but the human actions that flow from values, choice and commitment, and represent who and what we are.

In Chapter 3, I pointed out Ignatius of Loyola's intention to form the members of the Society of Jesus in a spirituality that found God in all things. In addition to the awareness which I have discussed earlier as a contemplative attitude toward life and the world, this spiritual stance leads to contemplative action in union with God's action. For Ignatius, union with God's will in all aspects of one's life was as real and as important a goal as union with God in prayer. In fact they were not different, but a desire and an awareness which were experienced in different modes of acting. David Lonsdale, S.J., has described this being contemplative-in-action as implying both surrender and commitment out of love.[6] From the contemplation of God's action in us and in the world, we surrender out of gratitude and love and offer our gifts in service to God's Kingdom. Commitment to finding and doing the will of God gives a direction to the whole of life and enables one to engage fully in life as one collaborates with God's action, with God's saving work in the world. For Lonsdale, this surrender and commitment are sparked and supported by finding God in contemplative prayer, but growth in union with God does not then necessarily mean more time for prayer, because engagement in the activities of life are not felt as taking one away from God.

Teilhard de Chardin, S.J., whose life and work were so intimately bound up with the world, expresses this sense of grace from his own experience. Chardin writes that God "awaits us every instant in our action, in the work of the moment. There is a sense in which he is at the tip of my pen, my spade, my brush, my needle—of my heart and of my thought."[7]

The apostle Paul, an extremely active and engaged minister, had the insight that "We are God's co-workers . . ." (1 Cor. 3:9). Coming to a deeper understanding of this truth through insights on human action from philosophy, anthropology and theology can assist contemporary ministers to develop a spirituality of action.

B. Ministerial Action

"The Father is at work in the world, and I go on working" (John 5:17). For Jesus, the Father is the creator, the one who is always actively involved in his creation, and Jesus' own mission was to share in God's action. He stresses his own desire to be one with his Father in several places in John's gospel. "I have come down from heaven not to do my own will but to do the will of him who sent me." (6:38) "My food is to do the will of him who sent me and to finish his work." (4:34). Jesus also sets this focus as criterion for his followers. "It is not those who say to me, 'Lord, Lord', who will enter the kingdom of heaven, but the person who does the will of my Father in heaven." (Mt. 7:21).

Early in his ministry as portrayed in the gospel of Luke, Jesus identifies his mission: "I must announce the good news of the reign of God, because that is why I was sent." (Lk. 4:43). As Paul VI points out in *Evangelii Nuntiandi* (On Evangelization in the Modern World), Jesus, the first evangelizer, proclaimed the reign of God not only by his tireless preaching, but also by the witness of his life and death and by the liberating actions and signs which accompanied his ministry. Christian disciples, who are invited to share in the mission of Jesus, are called as Jesus was to the proclamation of God's reign today through the witness of their daily lives, through word and action.

Paul VI calls the Church to the evangelization of culture. This challenges ministers to address the gap between the culture and the gospel. It is a mission of stewardship, of care and concern for God's people, whom he loves, and for the world which God has created. Ministerial action is a work of co-creation, which has as its goal the liberation, salvation and transformation that are signs of the Kingdom which Jesus came to announce.

The focus of ministry is the people of God, therefore ministry is mainly about relationships. It is enhanced by the contemplative awareness that seeks and discovers God in each person. It is exercised especially in the recognition of Jesus himself in the poor, the hungry, the sick and imprisoned, where he has told us he could be found. (Mt. 25:35-40) It is service to the Body of Christ in its extension throughout the world, and it involves a quality of presence to the members of that Body that only a spiritually alive minister can offer.

In presenting reflections on prayer in Chapter 4, I referred to William Shannon's exploration of the elements of monastic prayer: *lectio, meditatio, oratio* and *contemplatio*. Later on in his book, Shannon shares his conviction that these should conclude with a fifth aspect, which he calls "*operatio*." The reflection on the Word of God and the gift of the Presence of God should impel the praying person to loving action for the concerns of God and in union with God. Our history of spirituality is replete with persons such as Teresa of Avila, Ignatius of Loyola, Francis of Assisi, Vincent de Paul, Catherine of Genoa, and Louise de Marillac who were totally open and present to God in prayer in their own hearts, and totally present to and involved with God in others in intense activity. The demands of active apostolic ministry today also challenge us to a contemplative discovery of God *in* our work rather than to view engagement in activity as seeming to take us away from God. As E. Edward Kinerk, S.J., has suggested, "We are 'horizontal mystics': we look upon God through the mist of the world around us and we end by finding God in the mist."[8]

As stated previously, authentic human action is accomplished through awareness and freedom. Thomas Clarke has applied this insight to what is done in ministry in what he calls "responsive ministry." In this view, Clarke writes, ". . . our ministry will be effective to the degree that we help people become aware of what is really happening in their total behavior, and be gradually freed for a true and integral response to life."[9] The awareness and freedom of the minister evokes the awareness and freedom of those to whom they minister. In both, the result is the authentic development and action of the person.

One of the most important insights into ministry for me came from a statement of Father John Shea in a talk several years ago. He said, "Ministry is not to deliver services, but to empower people." This resonated with my own experience of how I had been ministered to in my life by persons who loved and cared and thus sparked me, empowered me. Ministers empower people by helping others to believe in God's love and care, to value themselves and their gifts, to discover their own role in promoting God's reign in their family, their work situation, community and world. Ministers do this by exercising their own gifts for the good of all, gifts of proclaiming the Good News, of healing, teaching, supporting, loving, caring, freeing, being with, listening and challenging growth in others. All these ways of serving are ways of revealing and discovering the presence and action of God, who is intimately involved in people's lives.

As a result of his experience in South America, Henri Nouwen in *¡Gracias!* shares another important aspect of ministerial action. Nouwen reflects that for a long time the focus of ministry was what the minister brought or did *for* others, especially in a missionary situation. A change in attitudes, according to Nouwen, now calls ministers to the key stance of gratitude as they *receive* the hidden gifts of those they wish to serve and "make these gifts visible to the community as a source of celebration . . . The true skill of ministry is to help fearful and often oppressed men and women become aware of their own gifts, by receiving them in gratitude."[10] The effects of such an attitude are significant in the life of ministers who come to know that in receiving the gifts of others, they are receiving God. "A grateful life is a life in which we come to see that the Lord himself is the gift. The mystery of ministry is that the Lord is to be found where we minister."[11] The spiritual vision which is necessary for such a contemplative approach to one's ministry demands prayer. ". . . through prayer we become aware of the life of God within us and it is this God within us who allows us to recognize the God among us."[12]

Robert L. Kinast has offered a perspective on a spirituality of lay ministry which he describes as "caring for society."[13] Using case studies, he argues for a "spirituality of engagement" in which life experiences are the source or starting point for the encounter with God. The engagement in real life situations leads the minister to reflection on the experience, which in turn leads to an identification with God's action in Scripture, and to prayer and sharing with others. The concerns and commitments of life give a direction to the whole of life. They are the source of spiritual growth as ministers find God in the stories of everyday experience and then discover the biblical parallels which enable them to make connections which are shared and celebrated.

Each of the perspectives on ministerial action which I have described support the conviction that prayer *and* action provide continuity in the experience of the minister. They are as Lozano concludes, ". . . phases of a circular movement."[14] The innate tension at times indicates their essential connectedness. The ambiguity of human life requires the focused attentiveness to what one is doing, in order to be both contemplative and active in all dimensions of the quest to be one with God's plan for the Kingdom.

C. Justice and Compassion in Action

Concern for social justice is an essential component of ministerial spirituality. In fact, the biblical term for human holiness is the same as the word for justice, mišpāt. The Synod of Bishops in 1971 reminded us that "Action on behalf of justice and participation in the transformation of the world fully appear to us as a constituitive dimension of the preaching of the Gospel."[15] The Scriptures portray God's concern and "preferential option" for the poor. The example and mission of Jesus to bring good news to the poor, proclaim liberty to captives and recovery of sight to the blind, provide a focus for ministry especially in our time, when people seem expendable and unjust systems abound. The focus on liberation from all forms of human misery may take the form of direct service to the suffering and marginalized, or may include efforts to alleviate conditions of suffering and injustice or to change structures which cause them. The challenge to take a prophetic stance is what Sandra Schneiders, I.H.M., calls "the public face of mysticism."

An authentic spirituality summons us to hear especially the cry of the poor and to commit ourselves and our resources in some way to a compassionate response. In an article in *America* magazine, Tom Clarke, S.J., outlined the variety of possible responses that might be made.[16] We are called to act *for* the poor and to preach the good news *to* the poor; some are called to walk *with* the poor, others to live and work *as* the poor, and in some places we are experiencing the Church of the poor where the gospel goes forth *from* the poor to evangelize the Church itself. Perhaps one of the most challenging aspects of ministry today is to discover ways to live and minister from the perspective of the poor.

Active involvement in the contemporary struggle for justice is both an expression of real human action, which I explored earlier in this chapter, and the fruit of contemplative prayer through which we are enabled to hear the cry of the poor in our hearts. There is an intimate connection between compassion and contemplation. In Thomas Merton's words, "There is no theology of prayer that is not a theology of compassion."

The gospels indicate that the source of Jesus' strength, his clarity about his mission, his energy for ministry was found in his hours of contemplative communion with his Father. This is also true for the contemporary minister as I have explained in previous chapters. But it is important to realize the connection contemplative awareness has with action that is truly compassionate. Henri Nouwen writes:

> Compassion is the fruit of solitude and the basis of all ministry. The purification and transformation that take place in solitude manifest themselves in compassion . . . It is in solitude that we realize that nothing human is alien to us . . . In solitude our heart of stone can be turned into a heart of flesh, . . . a closed heart into a heart that can open itself to all suffering people in a gesture of solidarity.[17]

Prayer that leads to self-knowledge and detachment also results in greater openness to God and to others. Union with God deepens our awareness of identification with all others who are brothers and sisters in God. This solidarity is the basis of compassion. William Johnston, S.J., in his comprehensive study of mysticism and religion, *The Inner Eye of Love,* considers compassion as mysticism in action. Johnston writes:

> . . . Christian compassion is the discovery of Christ in the suffering people of the world. This union or solidarity with the poor and oppressed is of the very essence of Christian mysticism.[18]

The interconnectedness of contemplation and compassion also holds true for its converse. Not only does true contemplation lead to compassion, but as Merton points out, true contemplation is out of the question for one who is not compassionate. "No man who ignores the rights and needs of others can hope to walk in the light of contemplation because his way has turned aside from truth, from compassion and therefore from God."[19]

Both contemplation and compassion demand that the focus be on the other, not the self. Both require a quality of personal presence and flow from the deep, inner resources of one's being. Both involve the whole person and can lead to the self-transcendence which marks true spiritual growth. Significantly, contemplation and compassion put one in touch with God, who has identified himself as "Yahweh, a God of tenderness and compassion." (Exodus 34:6)

D. A Contemporary Concern About Action

In the history of spirituality there has been the prevalence of two dangerous temptations: quietism, or the retreat into long periods of prayer instead of action, and activism, the plunge into action with no time or energy for prayer. Today the second of these, activism, is more prevalent, and perhaps this is comprehensible in view of the magnitude of human needs and the incessant demands on ministers. Therefore, in a program of spiritual formation for ministry, I think it is important to draw attention to this danger.

This chapter on human action pointed out the need for action to be performed in awareness and freedom. This implies that ministers befriend their actions, be reflective, make choices, be aware of their motives for acting, live more transparent lives where they are open to input from others and alert to signals of warning. The contemporary phenomenon of burnout is not alien to ministers. Commenting on a remark of Douglas Steere, Thomas Merton wrote:

> There is a pervasive form of contemporary violence. The rush and pressure of modern life are a form of its innate violence. To allow oneself to be carried away by a multitude of conflicting concerns, to surrender to too many projects, to want to help everyone in everything is to succumb to violence . . . . The frenzy of the activist . . . destroys his own inner capacity for peace. It destroys the fruitfulness of his own work, because it kills the root of inner wisdom which makes work fruitful.[20]

Much that has been said already in this book provides a perspective to counteract this type of activism. In particular, the development of the contemplative dimension of one's life and prayer is essential. So also is the concept of Church that calls for collaborative ministry where burdens are shared. The stress on authentic human action precludes frenzied and addictive behavior. Compassion and justice begin with an awareness of one's own need for compassion and a willingness to receive compassion from God and others. Effective, holy ministers through the ages have sought and allowed God to minister to them as they opened themselves to his presence in the mystical experiences of ministry and in the mysticism of prayer.

E. Reflection Activities

1. Following the form for prayer suggested at the conclusion of Chapter 3, pray a Scripture passage in which Jesus is involved in action. Some examples might be Mark 1:29-39 (a "day" in Jesus' life), John 4:1 ff. (Woman at the Well), Luke 10:38-42 (with his friends), John 6:1-15 (Feeding 5000), Mark 10:46-52 (curing blind man), Luke 4:18-29 (announcing his mission), Luke 19:1-10 (with Zaccheus), Matt. 26:20-30 (Last Supper), or choose your own favorite "action" passage. Be there, watch, listen. What does Jesus have to say to you about human action? How are you in the scene? Any new awareness?

2. After becoming quiet within, pray the following questions. Ask God to lead you: a) Where is the Kingdom of God happening *today*? Look at some area of your life or ministry through God's eyes. *Let the Lord tell you* what he sees there, where God is, what God is doing. Look at persons and places from God's perspective. Be open to surprise! b) What's going on in

this portion of the Kingdom? c) Where are you being invited to assist the growth? d) A Kingdom of love, of justice, of peace?

3. Use the model of pastoral theological reflection outlined in Chapter 1 and the Appendix of this book to reflect on a past experience of your ministry. a) Review the experience as it occurred. Get in touch with all aspects: the persons, the event, the circumstances, the environment, your involvement, your feelings. b) What were the significant contemporary cultural dimensions of the experience? Social, psychological, political, etc.? What values were involved? c) What in the Tradition speaks to this experience? What theological issues are relevant in this case? d) As these dimensions of the experience interact and become clearer, what new insights or convictions do you have? How will this affect your ministry in the future?

4. In the model of prayer from question 1, choose one scene in the gospels where Jesus is present to another in a compassionate way. *Be present there* yourself in contemplative openness. Don't reason or think so much about the incident, just *be there,* focus on Jesus, and let whatever happens happen. Some possible scenes are: Luke 13:10-17 (stooped woman), Mark 1:40-45 (leper), Luke 7:36-50 (woman at Simon's house). John 11 (death of Lazarus), Mark 5:25-34 (woman with hemorrhage).

5. a) How does your ministry reflect the ministry of Jesus? b) What situations today need new life? compassion? c) Where is your ministry challenging you to grow? d) Who needs what you have to share? e) Whom are you being called to empower?

6. a) Ask God to help you become aware of God's compassion to you in your own life experience. (Passages like Exodus 34:6, Isaiah 43:1-10 or Psalm 139 might be helpful places to begin.) b) Recall a time when you received compassion from another person. c) Recall an occasion when you were present to another in a compassionate way. d) What areas of your life now are inviting you to become a more compassionate person?

7. Spend some time in prayer with this question: In what ways do you think God might want to minister to you? Let God tell you!

F. Suggested Readings

Clarke, Thomas E., S.J., *Playing in the Gospel.* Kansas City: Sheed & Ward, 1986. (Especially Chapter 4.)

Foley, Gerald and Schmaltz, Timothy, *Connecting Faith and Life.* Kansas City: Sheed and Ward, 1987.

Haight, Roger, S.J., "Foundational Issues in Jesuit Spirituality." *Studies in the Spirituality of Jesuits* 19/4 (September 1987):1-61.

Kinast, Robert L., *Caring for Society,* Chicago: Thomas More Press, 1985.

Lozano, John M., "The Theology and Spirituality of the Apostolic Life," in *Ministerial Spirituality and Religious Life.* Chicago: Claret Center for Resources in Spirituality, 1986.

Nouwen, Henri J. M., "The Monk and the Cripple: Toward a Spirituality of Ministry." *America* (March 15, 1980): 205-210.

6

An Integrated Spirituality

A. The Process of Ongoing Conversion

The challenge of our human, spiritual lives is to become integrated persons. A spirituality for ministry is one which furthers our development in ways that enable us to become holy and whole. Our holiness, as Paul reminds us, (1 Thessalonians 4:7) is God's desire and God's work in us. We are, in the words of Bernard Lonergan, invited to "a fated acceptance of a vocation to holiness."[1] This acceptance and surrender is the effect of our awareness of God's great, unconditional love for us. The process is one of ongoing conversion, our gradual transformation as we live and pray and minister to and with one another.

Conversion has been described as a subtle "turning" more and more toward God. It involves a change of consciousness which provides an alternative vision or perspective on our life and our world. There are times when this may seem to be caused by a sudden impact, as William Johnston implies when he suggests that two conditions for conversion are a shock and a period of solitude. But the invitation is also present in the seemingly normal conditions of our everyday experience.

I have invited reflection previously on the quality and value of our human action when it is done in awareness and freedom. Yet the challenge to grow in awareness and *to be really free* is ongoing. It requires honest, attentive listening and authentic struggle before God in prayer and with God in activity. It is easy to agree that love ought to show itself in deeds, but how can we be sure we are really loving and growing as loving persons? We can opt for a just and countercultural life-style, but there are then decisions to be made daily as to how to be faithful to this vision.

The paradigm for our journey of conversion is the Paschal Mystery of Jesus. The disciple is called to die on one level in order to rise on another level, to enter into and live the experience of Jesus. This involves a willingness to let go of our control over our lives and to let God lead. It is an acknowledgement that, as Rahner has said, God is addressing us in every situation in our lives. It is much more God's work in us than what *we do,* yet it involves openness to God's Presence in everything and our willingness to respond to the small, and at times, great invitations in each moment. It involves conscious choices that are consistent with our vision of faith.

Living the Paschal Mystery as an inevitable dimension of discipleship involves the Cross. The goal is not self-fulfillment but self-transcendence, which comes through love and is often the effect of suffering. Suffering is not sought nor is it a value in itself. Yet it is precisely in moments of pain, disintegration and breakdown that there can be the possibility for reintegration and breakthrough. Crisis points in life, moments of frustration, disillusionment, darkness, finitude, rejection, etc., can be moments of grace. We are forced to stop, to come back to the source of our life, the roots of our faith, to recognize our finiteness and our dependence on God. We are stripped of our illusions and learn what our real security is and what really matters. We are united to the sufferings of Jesus and with the suffering of the Body of Christ throughout the world in this historical moment.

Spiritual writers of our day, as well as those who have preceded us, have spoken of the grace of the Cross in different ways. Teilhard de Chardin speaks of the "divinization of our passivities." James Fowler writes of the "sacrament of defeat." Bonhoeffer stresses the "cost of discipleship" and proclaims that there is no "cheap grace." John Futrell, S.J., writes of the passive purifications of our life as God's hollowing us so that we can rely more on God and less on our own resources. In his words:

> Growth in apostolic holiness is a life-time process of being hollowed out by the Lord so that his own life of love can fill us with his peace and joy, which will reach other people in proportion to the hollowing. The hollowing is for his presence. Only when all barriers of self-seeking and self-love in our lives and in our apostolic service have been let go can we be filled fully with his presence . . .[2]

The experience of darkness can be in our prayer or in our active lives, or as Constance Fitzgerald, O.Carm., has recently explored, it can be endemic to our culture, a kind of "societal dark night."[3] If we are going to reach a level of integration, we need to name our experience and stay with it in trust. The great virtue here is poverty of spirit. It involves obedience as we listen to where God is in what we are experiencing. It is often prayer in the darkness, in which we stay in faith and hope, learn to surrender, and allow ourselves to be broken open so that new life can emerge. Like the Emmaus disciples, we need to learn that the Cross is part of the story, but not the whole story. We can grow in union with God and in authentic freedom through this process of conversion, which Lonergan insists is possible when I fall in love with God who has loved me before I knew it. It is all God's doing!

B. Elements Which Aid Integration

As I have indicated, integration does not just happen by our living through different experiences. The more that ministers can be assisted in articulating their experience and in becoming more consciously reflective, the greater will be the degree of unity and meaning in their lives. The reflection questions and activities suggested at the conclusion of the preceding chapters are offered as a means to inculcate attitudes and methods of reflection. I will now indicate some specific elements of a spiritual life that should be presented to and explored with ministers in order that at least some of these could become valuable components of their personal lives. These elements are merely outlined here. It would be advantageous for the facilitator or instructor to become familiar with these through the available literature on each topic.

1. *Journaling*—This has been suggested as an ongoing part of the process of this book. Journaling can be very simple, or can be more detailed and complex, such as the method proposed by Ira Progoff in the *Life Context Workshop*. It can be a reflection on one's prayer, on one's daily life, or both. In spite of some initial hesitation or resistance, most people who are guided in the process of journaling find it beneficial. As one reflects in order to write, one taps into a deeper sub-conscious awareness, and in the act of writing, releases this awareness and brings it to consciousness. Very often it is at this deeper level that God is moving us, bringing clarity, and challenging us to grow. A journal can help us to notice patterns and can become a record of how God has been keeping his promises in our life. Soren Kierkegaard has noted that "our lives are lived forward and understood backwards." Journaling can be a tool which assists this self-understanding and contributes to the fuller integration of prayer and life.

2. *The Awareness Examen*—In 1972, George Aschenbrenner, S.J., promoted a contemporary understanding and adaptation of the examen taught by Ignatius Loyola. In his article "Consciousness Examen,"[4] he stresses the value of the daily process as a way to grow in awareness of God's invitations in one's life experiences, and indicates how this method is a form of discernment of spirits. The five steps in the examen: thanksgiving, prayer for the light of the Spirit, practical survey of actions, contrition and sorrow, and hopeful resolution for the future are all in the context of prayer. The goal is a deeper awareness of our identity before God in faith and a consciousness of the graces and invitations in every moment. It is a tool which can lead to a mysticism of action and service. Other Jesuit writers have expanded on Aschenbrenner's work and illustrated how the examen can be a profitable mode of theological reflection. Some of these articles will be listed at the conclusion of this chapter.

3. *Spiritual Direction*—There is a renewed contemporary interest in this very old tradition of spiritual guidance. Today it may be called "spiritual companioning" as persons agree to walk and share their faith journey with another. The director is primarily a listener and a co-discerner. The goals for the directee include articulation, awareness, clarification and at times, decision-making. Spiritual direction may be helpful as an ongoing support in one's life of faith, or as a process and relationship entered into at a specific time for a specific goal. It is important for those seeking to grow in prayer, for those in times of spiritual crisis, for those involved in choices or crucial decisions. It can prove very helpful to ministers to have someone with whom to reflect on their ministerial experience and its relationship to their own lives. Spiritual direction aims at assisting growth toward maturity in faith and the fullness of life Jesus promised.

4. *Discernment*—This is a "spiritual art," a quality, a habit, a virtue, and at times, a personal or communal process for decision-making. All of the elements just mentioned, journaling, the awareness examen and spiritual direction, can assist a person in developing a discerning heart. It requires reflection and sensitivity to the leading of the Spirit and the inner movements of affectivity developed over time. Ignatius' Rules for the Discernment of Spirits are helpful and have been made accessible and relevant for contemporary spirituality by writers like Aschenbrenner, John English, S.J., Thomas Green, S.J., and others. Discernment presupposes a willingness to be led by the Spirit as Jesus was. It is a unique mode of prayer that integrates both prayer and action and promotes growth in authentic

response to God. This attentiveness which results in discerned action supports the contemplation-in-action stance explored earlier in this book.

5. *Theological Reflection*—Chapter 1 discussed the importance of theological reflection and of pastoral theological reflection for Christian ministry. I would like to emphasize this value in this section of the book as an essential reflective element in assisting integration in the minister. The method of the Whiteheads is an excellent one to follow. However, there are variations on the model and other contemporary models. Ministers should be instructed in a model and practice using it in group exercises during the period of spiritual formation.

Ongoing theological reflection is essential for authentic ministry. In order to approach Jesus' total fidelity to the proclamation of the Reign of God, we must keep asking the questions: Where is the Lord in this existential situation? Where is God leading? What does the Gospel have to say to this concern, today in this time and place?

6. *Summary*—Each of the experiences outlined in this section has as one of its goals awareness and growth in self-knowledge. Other such tools are available today with a similar goal, such as: the Myers-Briggs Personality Inventory, the Enneagram, Focusing, and Dream Workshops. The approach and significance of these could also be shared in a formation program.

Most of the activities explored in this chapter initially have an inward movement, but it is crucial to realize that the purpose of the movement within is to be able also to move outward in a more authentic way, in responsiveness to God's Presence and leading both within and without.

C. Community

The primary concern in this book is to assist in formation for a contemporary spirituality for ministry. An essential element of Christian spirituality is community, and while that topic warrants a whole study in itself, it is important in rounding out this work to outline a few points. In particular, community forms a bridge between action and contemplation, and so taking time to reflect on the significance of community can also deepen the awareness of the interconnectedness of these spiritual realities. What follows is a brief reflection on community in the early Christian tradition, in the contemporary culture, and in the experience of present day ministers. Some of the reflection activities at the conclusion of this chapter will invite ministers into their own personal integration of the role of community in their lives.

1. Christian Tradition

Belief in a God who is Trinity of persons is a basic tenet of Christian faith. God is the name of the relationship in love of Father, Son and Spirit. John tells us that "God is love" (1 Jn. 4:8, 16), a statement which Michael and Kenneth Himes call "the most basic Christian metaphor for God."[5] The individual person, made in the image of the Triune God, is to find his or her own identity in relationship with others. So also the Church, the sacrament of Christ, is a communion of persons, the People of God, united in faith and in love. Chapter 2 made reference to Avery Dulles' most recent model of the Church as a "community of disciples," drawn from the New Testament reflection on Jesus' life and ministry and on the experience of the early Church. Jesus himself gathered the first disciples, formed them, and sent them out together, not singly, to proclaim the good news of the Kingdom. It is within community that Christians can live out the injunctions of Jesus to his followers: "By this shall all know that you are my disciples, that you love one another." (Jn. 13:35) "If I, your Lord and Master, have washed your feet, so should you wash one another's feet." (Jn. 13:14)

The early Church document, the *Didache,* described four essential dimensions of the life of the Church: preaching and teaching (*kerygma*), community (*koinonia*), prayer and liturgy (*leitourgia*), and service (*diaconia*). All these were involved in building up the Body of Christ, the Church. The various ministries of service were ministries to the community and flowed from the life of the community. Christians' communion with one another was itself a witness to God's love. Within community they could hold together the polarities of prayer and action. (Acts 2:42-47)

Subsequent centuries present a history of Church development which varies greatly at times from the idyllic picture given in *Acts.* However, the goal of Christian community remains an essential component of Christianity. The development of ministries also is understood only in relationship to the community. Gifts and charisms are given to individuals for the service of the Christian community. Historical and cultural realities determine the needs of the community and affect the development of ministries in response to the leading of the Spirit.

2. Community and Contemporary Culture

The social sciences have enlarged our contemporary understanding of the importance of relationships and of community in the lives of individuals. They have thus, perhaps inadvertently, supported the insights from theology and experience of Christians. In the article previously cited, the Himes brothers state the mutual enrichment of the individual and the community in a Christian view:

> The individual and the community give life to one another: as the individual is more truly intelligent and free, more truly human and so more completely self-gift, the network of relationships in which the individual exists is furthered and enriched; the broader and deeper that network of relationships, the more truly human the community and the individual. . . Each relationship brings with it responsibilities. In order to carry out responsibilities, rights arise. The fundamental responsibility is to give oneself away as perfectly as possible. The fundamental right is the right to do so.[6]

The deep human desire for relationships in which one can both share oneself and be enriched by the sharing of others is noted often in contemporary psychology and sociology, yet at the same time the great difficulty Americans have in forming and sustaining community is evident. The impact of modern culture has had devastating effects on the personal and societal capacity to build and maintain enduring commitments. Robert Bellah and his associates in their perceptive study, *Habits of the Heart,* point out how the "rampant individualism" of our American culture has resulted in the breakdown of familial, ecclesial and civic communities. Their call for a renewal of "communities of memory and of hope"[7] issues a crucial challenge to the Church, and impacts significantly on a spirituality for ministry.

Community can exist in many forms and individual persons can belong to several groups which provide significant relationships and a sharing of some dimension of life. It is important that expectations for community not be focused on one group of persons for all one's relational needs. Much of the dissatisfaction with community stems from unreal expectations or lack of awareness of the demands of authentic community. While more Americans are becoming aware that patterns of individualism and isolation in our culture do not satisfy for a meaningful life, many are unwilling to enter into the pain and struggle that are part of the growth into true community. This is true in family relationships, working situations and ecclesial groups. Community involves a quality of presence to one another, a willingness to share oneself, to be open and thus, at times, vulnerable, and a consistent involvement in the life of the community. When shared ideals and purpose are the basis for community, the experience of shared living can be a great source of support and energy. At the same time, community can challenge and issue a call to authenticity and to sacrifice of personal desires for the good of the whole community. A willingness to give as well as to receive is an essential requirement for those seeking the richness of community.

3. Community and Ministry

A colleague of mine, Dick Westley, quotes Martin Buber as saying, "We expect a theophany of which we know only the place. And the place? the place is called Community."[8] Westley uses Buber's insight himself to write of community as "the saving place." Ministers in the contemporary Church have the task of working to facilitate this saving place through their relationships, their service and their everyday lives. It is through awareness and perception of God's presence in their midst and by personal presence to others that ministers can assist people in the discovery of this revelation, this theophany. In a similar vein, Henri Nouwen states:

> Community develops where we experience that something significant is taking place *where we are.* It is the fruit of the intimate knowledge that we are together not because of a common need . . . but because we are called together to help make God's presence visible in the world. Only to the degree that we have this knowledge of God's call can we transcend our own immediate needs and point together to him who is greater than these needs.[9]

Christian community witnesses to God's Presence in the living out of gospel values. Loving, caring, serving and supporting lead to self-transcendence and on-going transformation of the members. In shared faith, prayer and work, pain and struggle, success and failure, joys and sorrows Christian community is the locus for God's saving actions. Our vision is expanded and our lives are enriched by the sharing and the challenges. The investment of oneself is both a privilege and a responsibility. Community, in its call to inter-dependence, is a place of personal, ongoing mutual formation and a witness to the coming of God's kingdom of love, peace and justice.

The Latin American theologian, Gustavo Gutierrez has written that:

> Community life cultivates receptivity for God's reign and also proclaims it; in this reception and proclamation a community builds itself up as a community.[10]

Gutierrez reflects on the basic Christian communities that have developed in the Third World. We are also experiencing in the United States the powerful effect of such small communities that not only vitalize the members themselves, but also give new life to the larger community of the Church. From his own experience Gutierrez points out the inter-relatedness of solitude and community. Solitude leads to the hunger for community, and the support of community is essential for one's own personal journey through the desert.

It is not so much *that* we live our lives together that is significant, but *how* we share life that can speak of the coming of the Kingdom in our midst. The actual experience is both difficult and rewarding. The authenticity of love, the reality of acceptance and belonging, the experience of forgiveness and reconciliation, all contribute to spiritual growth. The minister not only is called to facilitate this grace-filled environment, but is also energized by it for service. Ministers are invited into ministering to community, and also to ministering that flows from community.

There are situations today in which ministers are alone in their particular call to service. The dangers of isolation and loneliness are very real. Ministers should be encouraged to form a network of supportive relationships of peers, friends and family, and to make definite scheduled times for being with significant others, even when it entails distance and some time away from the ministry situation. Also, in their ministerial setting, ministers, as disciples and persons who are called to be Church, have as a primary task, building community where they are. Kinast writes of "occasion-centered communities"[11] which are formed in the midst of shared action. In his analysis of the role of lay ministers in the Church in the present and in the future, he defines the role as "caring for society," and he suggests that the effect will be the formation of "communities of those who care." Contemporary cultural realities challenge ministers to be creative in response to the possibilities for community.

Prayer is an important element of Christian community. The community will benefit from the contemplative prayer of the individual members, but the prayer of the community is also essential. Liturgical prayer is a prime source of a community's life. Both in liturgy and apart from liturgy, shared reflection on the Word of God in Scripture is key to the community's life and mission. Contemplation of the Word leads community members to call one another to faithfulness to the Word in action. In this sense, community is a link between prayer and action.

Communal prayer also flows from reflection on the ministerial action. Intercession is a natural response to the needs of others. Thanksgiving and praise reflect awareness of God's working in both ministry and community. Discernment in prayer is a necessity for determining direction for further action. Presence to one another and to God in communal prayer enables each member of the community to be a beneficial Christian presence wherever they are.

This section began with the idea that our vocation to Christian community came from our relationship to our Triune God. Trinitarian life is one of mutual self-gift in love. What does this call us to as we attempt to live in love and praise of our God? Robert Imbelli suggests that it means:

> celebrating the common life of God and contributing to the common life of humankind. Christian contemplation and action, Christian worship and mission, Christian sacrament and sacrifice all conspire toward their fulfillment in the blessed Name of the Triune God. From this Name they derive their inspiration: in this Name they achieve their integration—the in-breathing and out-breathing of trinitarian Presence. In this Presence we are no longer strangers and aliens. We receive the freedom of the city and become fellow citizens of the saints.[12]

D. Reflection Activities

1. Choose a scripture passage that was significant for you in your past or present experience, at a particular moment of decision or a critical time. Be there, enter into the Presence of the Lord into the scene from the Gospel or whatever setting. Let the moment unfold again. What was the focus? Recall your feelings, the emotions associated with the time. What did you experience? learn? share with the Lord? What did you have to lose? What have to let go? What change or movement occurred within you? What did you gain? How were you enriched? Were you aware of a movement from unfreedom to

liberation or healing? How was the Lord with you? How present? What did your heart know?

Stay there with the Lord and share your present feelings with him. Return to the Scripture passage. Does it still speak to you today? Is it where you are? Do you have any new insights or convictions?

Write down some of your reflections after this prayer time.

2. We say that our Christian life is one of ongoing conversion, of living out the Paschal Mystery of dying and rising. Recall a period of time in your life that you now see as a real conversion experience. Reflect on the process as you experienced it. Can you name the growth and new life you experienced? Where is God inviting you to grow now? What is the cutting edge?

3. Read the article on "Consciousness Examen" by George Aschenbrenner, S.J. Practice using a condensed form of the Examen with the five steps mentioned for several days, or over a few weeks. Share the effects of this practice. Notice if there is growth in awareness of God's moving and invitation in your life.

4. What are your main supports for your ministerial life? From what "wellsprings" do you draw refreshment? Are there untapped resources you might explore?

5. What communities or groups do you belong to now? How do you experience the need for support from community? How has community assisted your spiritual growth? How has community supported your outreach in ministry? Are there any further steps you might take regarding your participation in community?

6. Pray one of the following passages from Scripture: Psalm 138, Psalm 118, Isaiah 54:9-10, Ephesians 3:14-21. As you become aware of the blessings and gifts of your life, let your heart respond to God in gratitude and love.

7. Jesus said "I have come that they might have life and have it to the full." (John 10:10) In prayer share with the Lord your

desires for this fullness of life. Ask to see the obstacles to that fullness in you. Listen to what God wants to do for you, to be for you. Let God tell you!

E. Suggested Readings

1. *Conversion*

Constance Fitzgerald, O.C.D., "Impasse and Dark Night," in *Living With Apocalypse: Spiritual Resources for Social Compassion*, ed. Tilden Edwards, New York: Harper & Row, 1984.

John Futrell, S.J., "Growing Older Gracefully," *Human Development* 3, No. 3, Fall, 1982.

Thomas M. Green, S.J., *When the Well Runs Dry*, Notre Dame, Ind.: Ave Maria Press, 1979.

William Johnston, S.J., *The Inner Eye of Love*, San Francisco: Harper & Row, 1978.

Paul V. Robb, S.J., "Conversion as a Human Experience," *Studies in the Spirituality of Jesuits*, May, 1982.

2. *Reflectivity*

George A. Aschenbrenner, S.J., "Consciousness Examen," *Review for Religious* 31, No. 1 January, 1972.

John Haughey, S.J., "Hindsight, Prayer and Compassion," in *Living With Apocalypse* ed. Tilden Edwards, New York: Harper & Row, 1984.

Donald St. Louis, "The Ignatian Examen: A Method of Theological Reflection." *The Way*, Supplement No. 55, Spring, 1986.

3. *Community*

Gerald Foley & Timothy Schmaltz, *Laity in Community: Holiness of Ordinary Life*. Kansas City: Sheed & Ward, 1988.

Gustavo Gutierrez, *We Drink From Our Own Wells*. Maryknoll, N.Y.: Orbis Books, 1984.

Robert L. Kinast, *Caring for Society*. Chicago: Thomas More Press, 1985.

Evelyn E. Whitehead and James D. Whitehead, *Community of Faith*, The Seabury Press, N.Y., 1982.

7
Conclusion

The purpose of this work was to provide a tool for the process of formation in a spirituality for contemporary active ministry. The main focus was to explore the contemplation/action dynamics of ministerial life using a method of pastoral theological reflection.

Chapter 1 provided a foundation for the book and indicated significant insights of Lonergan and Tracy and the method of pastoral theological reflection of the Whiteheads. Chapter 2 clarified concepts and terms that seemed essential to the particular topic to be developed.

Chapter 3 discussed the action/contemplation issue and the attempt to hold both these poles in creative tension in the history of Christian spirituality. It focused on the dynamic of prayer and ministry in the life of Jesus, and looked at some facets of the question today. Chapters 4 and 5 explored each aspect of the issue, Prayer and Contemplation in 4 and Action and Ministry in 5. Chapter 6 pointed out the need for integration, and suggested three essential components of integration: the personal, ongoing conversion process, aids for reflecting on one's experience, and the role of Christian community.

The suggestions in each chapter for personal reflection, prayer and journaling, provide a means for using this book to integrate the ideas presented into the minister's own experience of faith and spirituality.

In various ways throughout, the tension between contemplation and action has been expressed as something that (a) is necessary, and (b) can be looked at creatively. Neither one pole nor the other is more important in the spirituality of the minister. Rather, both poles are essential. As stressed in Chapter 4, prayer, and especially contemplative prayer, is a crucial element of Christian ministerial spirituality. However, as demonstrated in Chapter 5, human action which is performed in awareness and freedom, in union with God's action and plan for the Kingdom, must also flow from the contemplative dimension of the minister's life. The goal is union with God in prayer *and* action. The movement is circular, the connection is essential. A program of formation in a spirituality for ministry will be effective only if it focuses on both prayer and ministry, and to the degree that it provides opportunities for reflection and integration on the part of the participants. I hope that the method used in this book, the insights that are developed, and the reflection activities offered, will prove a useful tool in such an important process.

Other aspects of contemporary ministerial spirituality could be pursued according to this method. Some important ones that have received only brief attention are:

- a life-style for ministry today;
- the impact of contemporary culture and the counter-cultural position;
- further exploration of community and spirituality.

The scope of this book is necessarily limited. I encourage others to continue the quest for other dimensions of a contemporary ministerial spirituality.

Appendix

Theological Method and Pastoral Theological Reflection

Bernard Lonergan's work on method in theology defines method as "a normative pattern of recurrent and related operations yielding cumulative and progressive results."[1] It is meant to be a framework which allows for creativity and intelligence and provides a structure for conversation and synthesis. Lonergan refers to his own method as a Transcendental Method which has as its object the heightening of awareness as to what one is already doing. His transcendental precepts or imperatives are: "Be attentive, be intelligent, be reasonable, be responsible."[2] The conscious operations involved in this heightening of awareness are experiencing, understanding, judging and deciding.[3]

Lonergan's method is empirical, that is, it originates in experience, and as a theological transcendental method, it is rooted in the faith experience of "being-in-love with God."[4] This "Being-in-love without restriction" is recognized as the gift of God which calls us toward the fulfillment of our capacity for self-transcendence. Thus, "Faith is the knowledge born of religious love,"[5] and it comes through the process of conversion. Lonergan defines religious conversion as:

> Being grasped by ultimate concern. It is total and permanent self-surrender without conditions, qualifications, reservations. But it is such a surrender, not as an act, but as a dynamic state that is prior to and principle of subsequent acts. It is . . . a fated acceptance of a vocation to holiness.[6]

The progression, if it is helpful to attempt an expression of reality, is from an experience of God's love leading to being-in-love, to the total conversion to God of one's whole self, in response to God's initiative. The awareness of this experience leads to faith and toward self-transcendence. The gift of God's love is what Lonergan calls the "Inner Word," and the

"Outer Word" is the religious tradition which comes from God through the community of faith. It is through the heightened awareness in the transcendental method of being attentive, intelligent, reasonable and responsible that we can name this experience.

Lonergan's insights are a rich source for reflection on Christian spirituality. In his words, "He made us in his image, for our authenticity consists in being like him, in self-transcending, in being origins of value, in true love."[7]

David Tracy speaks of the common denominator of what he calls our "post-Christian" and "post-modern" society as the search for "the full affirmation of the ultimate significance of our lives in this world."[8] This is the secular or cultural faith in the final worth of our lives here and now. Tracy's conviction is that it is the theologians' task to illuminate how "a proper understanding of the explicitly Christian faith can render intellectually coherent and symbolically powerful that common secular faith which we share."[9] His conclusion, in which he concurs with Lonergan, is that this is a demand for self-transcendence, and he values Lonergan's transcendental precepts as a very helpful articulation of a method.

Tracy states the two main sources of theology to be our common human experience and language, and the Christian tradition. In order to elaborate a method for theology dealing with these two sources, he subscribes to the prior need for a model. For Tracy, theological models are disclosive. They don't provide exact pictures of realities, but disclose or re-present what they interpret. Tracy calls his own model a Revisionist Model. It involves a critical correlation of the meanings present in common experience and of the meanings present in the Christian Texts.[10]

Since both the contemporary situation and the Christian tradition are mediated to us through language and symbol, Tracy insists on the need for interpretation of both.[11] In his words, the "permanent achievements" of the tradition "can and must be won, over and over again, by a contemporary commitment to a hermeneutics of restoration."[12]

He insists on a "critical" correlation of the two sources of theology, 1) The texts of the Tradition and 2) Common human experience, explaining the positive aspects of the concept as "a fidelity to open-ended inquiry, a loyalty to defended mythological canons, a willingness to follow the evidence wherever it leads."[13] The correlations are between the questions and answers of both sources, the Christian tradition and the contemporary situation, in order to determine their similarities and differences and their truth value.

Tracy describes the central symbol of the Christian fact as "the event and person of Jesus Christ as the decisive disclosure of the Christian construal of God, self and world."[14]

Tracy believes that a revisionist model of "mutually critical correlation" calls for a transcendental or metaphysical method of reflection. He refers to various attempts to show how a religious dimension is present in our everyday experience and language: the existentialists' attention to both anxiety and basic trust, Tillich's "ultimate concern" in all human activity, and Lonergan's analysis of religious experience as "a being-in-love-without-qualification." For his part, Tracy proposes his method as a metaphysical study of the cognitive claims of religion and theism as an integral part of the theologian's task.

The contribution of the methods of Lonergan and Tracy as outlined here are part of what is termed fundamental theology. I would like to use them as the backdrop against which to view a brief exploration of practical theology or what we also call pastoral theology, with a view to outlining a method for deepening our comprehension of the elements of a contemporary spirituality.

A Method of Pastoral Theological Reflection

Lonergan states that "practical theology is concerned with the effective communication of Christ's message."[15] For Tracy, the task of practical theology is "to test the [Christian] vision and, in that testing, transform it."[16] Practical theology then, or pastoral theological reflection, is concerned with ministry. Supported by the foundation of theological methods, it proceeds to a critical reflection on what we do when we act pastorally. It is a "critical reflection" in that it involves a willingness to be self-critical, an awareness of one's method and presuppositions, and a willingness to revise one's perspective under certain conditions.[17]

In a period of complexity and pluralism, with many competing voices and new questions continually facing those engaged in ministry, it is important that decisions flow from a method that allows us to be both responsible and faithful to our tradition and to one another.

In *Method in Ministry,* the Whiteheads present both a model and a method for theological reflection in Christian ministry. Drawing on the expertise of Lonergan, Tracy and many others, they offer a coherent and integrated approach to pastoral reflection which they present as "a systematic way to approach the various sources of religious information, one that leads not just to theoretical insight, but to pastoral decision."[18]

First, I would like to look at the Whiteheads' tripolar model.[19] It focuses on the three main sources of religiously significant information for pastoral reflection, decision and action. These sources are: Christian tradition, personal experience and information from the contemporary culture. By the Christian tradition is meant not only the basic Scriptures of the tradition, but also the history of the Christian Church and the "sensus fidelium," the sense of faith in the Christian community which has perdured through the centuries and is viable today through the action of the Holy Spirit.

In the category of personal experience is included the experience of the individual minister and the experience of the specific community. We have seen how theologians today place a high priority on personal experience as a privileged locus for God's activity. In their model the Whiteheads take Tracy's category of "common human experience," which includes both the personal and the cultural dimension, and separate it into two categories.

By the cultural information the Whiteheads mean "that sort of understanding, conviction, or bias in the culture which contributes explicitly or implicitly to any theological reflection in ministry."[20] This influence from the culture may be a positive or negative influence in the field of pastoral activity. It includes understandings of the human person and of society which are learned from philosophy, psychology, social sciences, political theory and other religious traditions.

The use of this tri-polar model provides the resources needed for pastoral theological reflection. They are the starting point for the process involved in the Whiteheads' method of theological reflection which leads to pastoral decisions and action. This method is a "critical correlation" in Tracy's words, of the three sources of information using a three-step process: attending, assertion, decision.

The initial stage of attending involves listening in an active, open way to the three sources of information as they are relevant to the pastoral issue being addressed. Attending to the Tradition involves, as Karl Rahner has suggested, both befriending the Tradition, becoming more familiar with it, and distancing oneself from it in order to more freely critique it. The minister and the community need to grow in appreciation and interpretation of both the texts of Scripture and the historical development of the Tradition. Attending to personal experience means developing interpersonal skills to hear accurately the story and to discern the needs of those to whom ministry is directed. It also involves the art of sensitive listening to oneself, to one's inner feelings, intuitions and convictions, and attention to the experience of the community in which the pastoral ministry is exercised. Attending to the cultural information involves research and questioning in the various fields of knowledge that could shed light on the issue, as well as listening to the unique cultural setting of the community.

The stage of assertion is when the information from these three sources is engaged in a process of mutual clarification and challenge in order to expand understanding and deepen insight concerning the topic or pastoral issue. Putting the three poles of the model into relationship or mutual dialogue is what David Tracy calls "mutually critical correlation."

When the investigation and correlation of the information yields a new perspective or understanding, then the third stage of the method is decision making for responsible pastoral action.

As persons involved in ministry today, we must also be engaged in theology, in touch with the experience of people in today's unique moment of history and of culture, and aware of what is going on in our own religious journey. I believe we must not only be engaged in theological reflection ourselves, but should encourage those with whom we minister to reflect on their experience in the light of the Christian tradition, in order that all may grow, both in self-knowledge, and in the wisdom of how to live the gospel and share it wherever they are. The Whiteheads have provided a method of pastoral reflection, correlation and decision-making that is valid for the wide range of issues we face.

Endnotes

Chapter 1

1. Bernard J. F. Lonergan, S.J., *Method in Theology,* (New York: Herder and Herder, 1972).

2. David Tracy, *A Blessed Rage for Order,* (New York: The Seabury Press, 1975).

3. *Ibid.,* p. 4.

4. Charles V. Gerkin, *Widening The Horizons,* (Philadelphia: The Westminister Press, 1986), p. 61.

5. James D. and Evelyn E. Whitehead, *Method in Ministry,* (New York: The Seabury Press, 1980).

Chapter 2

1. Harvey D. Egan, S.J., "Mysticism and Karl Rahner's Theology," in *Theology and Discovery: Essays in Honor of Karl Rahner, S.J.,* ed. William J. Kelly, S.J., (Milwaukee: Marquette University Press, 1980), p. 148.

2. *Ibid.,* p. 141.

3. Karl Rahner, S.J., *Foundations of Christian Faith,* (New York: The Seabury Press, 1978), p. 11.

4. cf. Karl Rahner, S.J., "Reflections on the Experience of Grace," *Theological Investigations,* Vol. III, pp. 86-90 as summarized in Egan, p. 155.

5. George A. Aschenbrenner, S.J., "Active and Monastic: Two Apostolic Lifestyles," *Bulletin of International Union of Superiors General,* No. 70 (1986), p. 5.

6. David Lonsdale, S.J., "Fostering Spiritual Growth" in *Can Spirituality Be Taught?,* eds. Jill Robson and David Lonsdale, (London: Association

of Centres of Adult Theological Association and British Council of Churches, 1988), p. 82.

7.   Robert N. Bellah, et al., *Habits of the Heart*, (Berkeley: University of California Press, C. 1985; reprint ed., New York: Harper & Row, Perennial Library, 1986).

Chapter 3

1.   Theophane the Monk, *Tales of a Magic Monastery*, (New York: Crossroad, 1981), p. 42.

2.   William R. Callahan, S.J., "Spirituality and Justice: An Evolving Vision of the Great Commandment," in *Contemporary Spirituality: Responding to the Divine Initiative*, ed. Francis A. Eigo, O.S.A. (Villanova, Pa.: Villanova University Press, 1983), p. 50.

3.   Jon Sobrino, S.J., *Christology at the Crossroads*, (Maryknoll: Orbis Books, 1978), p. 175.

4.   Gregory the Great, "Homiliae in Ezechielem," quoted by Santiago G. Silva, in "Overcoming the Antimony Action—Contemplation," in *Ministerial Spirituality and Religious Life*, Lozano, et al., (Chicago: Claret Center for Resources in Spirituality, 1986), p. 51.

5.   George A. Lane, S.J., *Christian Spirituality*, (Chicago: Loyola University Press, 1984), p. 25.

6.   *Ibid.*, p. 24.

7.   Quoted by Regis J. Armstrong, O.F.M. Cap. and Ignatius C. Brady, O.F.M., in *Francis and Clare: The Complete Works*, (New York: Paulist Press, 1982), p. 115.

8.   *Ibid.*, p. 139.

9.   *Ibid.*, p. 140.

10.   Kenneth Smits, Capuchin, "Franciscan Living: An Ecology of Prayer, Community and Ministry," *The New Round Table* 37, (Spring 1984): 83.

11.   Maurice Guiliani, S.J., "Finding God in All Things," in *Finding God in All Things*, trans. by William J. Young, S.J., (Chicago: Henry Regnery Co., 1958), p. 3.

12.   *Ibid.*, p. 11.

13.   *Ibid.*, p. 22-23.

14.   Harvey D. Egan, S.J., *Ignatius Loyola the Mystic*, (Willington: Michael Glazier, 1987), p. 126.

15.   James D. Whitehead, p. 156-7.

Chapter 4

1.   Sr. M. Corita Clarke, R.D.C., "The Paradoxes of Prayer." *Living Prayer* 19 (September - October 1986): pp 12-13.

2.   The use of the masculine form of pronoun in referring to God is merely a case of conformity to conventional usage. It has no significance beyond the restrictions of language structure.

3.   Abraham Heschel, *The Prophets*, vol. II (San Francisco: Harper and Row, 1962), p. 267.

4.   Thomas Merton, quoted in article by David Steindal-Rast, "Man of Prayer," in *Thomas Merton, Monk*, ed. Bro. Patrick Hart (New York: Doubleday, Image Books, 1976) p. 80.

5.   Anthony de Mello, S.J. *Sadhana: A Way to God*, (St. Louis): The Institute of Jesuit Sources, 1979).

6.   Pedro Arrupe, S.J. *"Five Recent Documents from Father General Pedro Arrupe, S.J. on Spirituality for Today's Jesuits."* (New Orleans: Southern Printing Co., 1980) p. 3.

7.   Thomas Keating, *Open Mind, Open Heart*, (New York: Amity House, 1986).

8.   Karl Rahner, *Theological Investigations*, vol. VII: Further Theology of the Spiritual Life I, trans. David Bourke (New York: Herder and Herder, 1971), p.15.

9.   Aschenbrenner, p.13

Chapter 5

1.   Thomas E. Clarke, S.J., *Playing in the Gospel,* (Kansas City: Sheed & Ward, 1986).

2.   *Ibid.,* p.61.

3.   *Ibid.,* p.64.

4.   *Ibid.,* p.67.

5.   Roger Haight, S.J., "Foundational Issues in Jesuit Spirituality," *Studies in the Spirituality of Jesuits* 19/4 (September 1987): 1-61.

6.   David Lonsdale, S.J., "Contemplative in Everyday Life," *The Way Supplement* 59 (Summer 1987): pp. 77-87.

7.   Pierre Teilhard de Chardin, S.J., *The Divine Milieu,* (New York: Harper & Row, 1960) p.64.

8.   E. Edward Kinerk, S.J., "When Jesuits Pray: A Perspective on the Prayer of Apostolic Persons," *Studies in the Spirituality of Jesuits* 17/5 (November 1985) p.12.

9.   Thomas E. Clarke, p.68.

10.   Henri J. M. Nouwen, *¡Gracias!,* (San Francisco: Harper & Row, 1983), p.19.

11.   *Ibid.,* p.20.

12.   *Ibid.,* p.21.

13.   Robert L. Kinast, *Caring for Society,* (Chicago: The Thomas More Press, 1985), pp. 141-151.

14.   Lozano, p.30.

15.   Synod of Bishops, *Justice in the World,* No. 6. (Washington, D.C.: United States Catholic Conference, 1971).

16.   Thomas E. Clarke, S.J., "Option for the Poor: A Reflection," *America,* (January 30, 1988): pp. 95-99.

17.   Henri Nouwen, *The Way of the Heart,* (New York: The Seabury Press, 1981) pp.33-34.

18.   William Johnston, *The Inner Eye of Love,* (San Francisco: Harper & Row, 1978) p.13.

19.   Thomas Merton, *New Seeds of Contemplation*, (New York: New Directions Publishing Corporation, 1962) pp.18-19.

20.   Thomas Merton, source unknown, but quoted for its great relevance and perception.

Chapter 6

1.   Lonergan, p. 240.

2.   John Futrell, S.J., "Growing Older Gracefully," *Human Development* 3, No. 3 (Fall 1982): 12.

3.   Constance Fitzgerald, O.C.D., "Impasse and Dark Night," in *Living with Apocalypse,* ed. Edward H. Tilden (San Francisco: Harper & Row, 1984).

4.   George Aschenbrenner, S.J., "Consciousness Examen." *Review for Religious* 31, No. 1 (January 1972).

5.   Michael J. Himes and Kenneth R. Himes, "Human Rights, Economics, and the Trinity." *Commonweal,* March 14, 1986, p.138.

6.   *Ibid.,* p.139.

7.   Bellah, et al., pp.152-155.

8.   Martin Buber, quoted in Dick Westley, *A Theology of Presence* (Mystic, Ct.: Twenty-Third Publications, 1988), p.64.

9.   Nouwen, *¡Gracias!,* p.66.

10.   Gustavo Gutierrez, *We Drink From Our Own Wells* (Maryknoll, N.Y.: Orbis Books, 1984), p.133.

11. Kinast, p.156.

12. Robert Imbelli, "Trinitarian Politics," *Review for Religious* 48 (March/April 1989): 233.

Appendix

1. Lonergan, p. 4.

2. *Ibid.*, pp. 13-14, p. 18, 20.

3. *Ibid.*, p. 14.

4. *Ibid.*, p. 106.

5. *Ibid.*, p. 115.

6. *Ibid.*, p. 240.

7. *Ibid.*, p. 117.

8. Tracy, *Rage*, p. 8.

9. *Ibid.*, p. 9.

10. *Ibid.*, pp. 46-56.

11. David Tracy, "The Foundations of Practical Theology," in *Practical Theology: The Emerging Field in Theology, Church and World*, ed. Don Browning, (New York: Harper & Row, 1983), p. 63.

12. Tracy, *Rage*. p. 12.

13. *Ibid.*, p. 7.

14. Tracy, "Foundations," p. 64.

15. Lonergan, *Ibid.*, p. 362.

16. Tracy, "Foundations," p. 72.

17. James N. Poling and Donald E. Miller, *Foundations for a Practical Theology of Ministry*, (Nashville, Tenn.: Abingdon Press, 1985), p. 32.

18. Whiteheads, p.2.

19. *Ibid.*, Chapter 1, pp. 11-26.

20. *Ibid.*, pp. 12-13.

Bibliography

Apostolic Exhortation, *On Evangelization in the Modern World, (Evangelli Nuntiandi)* Pope Paul VI, December 8, 1975. United States Catholic Conference, 1976.

Arrupe, Pedro, S.J. *Five Recent Documents from Father General Pedro Arrupe, S.J. on Spirituality for Today's Jesuits.* New Orleans: Southern Printing Co. 1980.

Aschenbrenner, George A., S.J. "Active and Monastic: Two Apostolic Lifestyles." *Bulletin of International Union of Superiors General* no. 70 (1986): 4-17.

_____ "Come, Let us Talk This Over: Issues in Spirituality, 1985—" *Review for Religious* 44 (July/ August 1985): 571-90.

_____ "Consciousness Examen," *Review for Religious* 31, No.1, (January 1972): 14-21.

Au, Wilkie, S.J., Ph.D. "Understanding Lay Ministry." *Human Development* 8 (Winter 1987): 33-38.

Baum, Gregory. *Man Becoming: God in Secular Language.* New York: Herder and Herder, 1970.

Bellah, Robert N.; Madsen, R.; Sullivan, W.M.; Swidler, A.; and Tipton, S.M. *Habits of the Heart.* Berkeley : University of California Press, c. 1985; reprint ed., New York: Harper & Row, Perennial Library, 1986.

Caligiuri, Angelo M. "Spirituality and Ordinary Human Experience." *Review for Religious* 37 (May 1978): 454-60.

Cameli, Louis John. "Spirituality: a Supplement to the Handbook." *Chicago Studies* 20. no. 2 (Summer 1981): 177-190.

Clarke, Sister M. Corita, R.D.C. "Compassion: A Spirituality for Today." *Review for Religious* 37, (July 1978): 516- 32.

_____"The Paradoxes of Prayer." *Living Prayer* 19 (September - October 1986): 12-13.

Clarke, Thomas E., S.J. "Option for the Poor: A Reflection," *America,* January 30, 1988, 95-99.

_____*Playing in the Gospel.* Kansas City: Sheed & Ward, 1986.

de Mello, Anthony, S.J. *Sadhana: A Way To God.* Study Aids on Jesuit topics, no.9 in series IV. St. Louis: The Institute of Jesuit Sources, 1979.

_____*Wake UP! Spirituality for Today.* (Video Cassette Program - 3 cassettes) Allen, Texas: Tabor Publishing, 1987.

_____*A Way To God Today.* (Video Cassette Program - 6 cassettes.) Allen, Texas: Tabor Publishing, 1985.

Dreyer, Elizabeth. "Tradition and Lay Spirituality." *Spirituality Today* 39 (Autumn 1987): 196-210.

Edwards, Tilden. *Living in the Presence.* San Francisco: Harper & Row, 1987.

Egan, Harvey D., S.J. *Ignatius Loyola the Mystic.* The Way of the Christian Mystics series, vol. 5. Wilmington: Michael Glazier, 1987.

_____"Mysticism and Karl Rahner's Theology." In *Theology and Discovery: Essays in Honor of Karl Rahner, S.J.* pp 139-58. Edited by William J. Kelly, S.J. Milwaukee: Marquette University Press, 1980.

Eigo, Francis A., O.S.A., ed. *Contemporary Spirituality: Responding to the Divine Initiative.* Villanova, Pa.: Villanova University Press, 1983.

Fitzgerald, Constance, O.C.D. "Impasse and Dark Night." In *Living with Apocalypse: Spiritual Resources for Social Compassion,* ed. Tilden Edwards, New York: Harper & Row, 1984.

Francis of Assisi, St., and Clare, St. *Francis and Clare: the Complete Works.* Translation and introduction by Regis J. Armstrong, O.F.M. Cap. and Ignatius C. Brady. O.F.M. New York: Paulist Press, 1982.

Futrell, John, S.J. "Growing Older Gracefully." *Human Development* 3, No. 3, (Fall 1982): 6-12.

Galilea, Segundo. *Following Jesus.* Maryknoll: Orbis Books, 1981.

Gannon, Thomas M., S.J., and Traub, George W., S.J. *The Desert and the City.* New York: Macmillan, 1969; reprint ed. Chicago: Loyola University Press, 1984.

Gerkin, Charles V. *Widening the Horizons.* Philadelphia: The Westminster Press, 1986.

Green, Thomas M., S.J. *Come Down Zacchaeus.* Notre Dame, Ind: Ave Maria Press, 1988.

_____*When the Well Runs Dry.* Notre Dame, Ind.: Ave Maria Press, 1979.

Gutierrez, Gustavo. *We Drink From Our Own Wells.* Maryknoll, N.Y.: Orbis Books, 1984.

Haight, Roger, S.J. "Foundational Issues in Jesuit Spirituality." *Studies in The Spirituality of Jesuits* 19/4 (September 1987): 1-61.

Hall, Thelma, r.c. *Too Deep for Words.* Mahwah, N.J.: Paulist, 1988.

Hart, Brother Patrick, ed. *Thomas Merton, Monk.* New York: Doubleday, Image Books, 1976.

Helminiak, Daniel A. *Spiritual Development.* Chicago: Loyola University Press, 1986.

Heschel, Abraham. *The Prophets.* 2 vols. San Francisco: Harper & Row, 1962.

Himes, Michael J. and Himes, Kenneth R. "Human Rights, Economics, and the Trinity." *Commonweal,* March 14, 1986, pp.137-141.

Imbelli, Robert. "Trinitarian Politics," *Review for Religious* 48 (March/April 1989): 230-233.

Johnson, Ann Therese Searing. "The Spirituality of the Minister." A project submitted for the degree Doctor of Ministry, Andover Newton Theological School, Newton Center, Mass., 1986.

Johnston, William. *The Inner Eye of Love.* San Francisco: Harper & Row, 1978.

Keating, Thomas. *Open Mind, Open Heart.* New York: Amity House, 1986.

Kinast, Robert L. *Caring for Society.* Chicago: The Thomas More Press, 1985.

Kinerk, E. Edward, S.J. "When Jesuits Pray: A Perspective on the Prayer of Apostolic Persons." *Studies in the Spirituality of Jesuits* 17/5 (November 1985).

Lane, George A., S.J. *Christian Spirituality.* Chicago: Loyola University Press, 1984.

Leckey, Dolores R. *Laity Stirring the Church.* Philadelphia: Fortress Press, 1987.

Lonergan, Bernard J.F., S.J. *Method in Theology.* New York: Herder and Herder, 1972.

Lonsdale, David. "Contemplative in Everyday Life." *The Way Supplement* 59 (Summer 1987): 77-87.

Lozano, John M. C.M.F., Bergant, D., Schniller, J.P., Moore, M.E., Carretto, C., and De Luca, G. *Ministerial Spirituality and Religious Life.* Religious Life Series. Chicago: Claret Center for Resources in Spirituality, 1986.

Mc Brien, Richard P. *Ministry.* New York: Harper & Row, 1987.

May, Gerald. "To Bear the Beams of Love: Contemplation and Personal Growth." *The Way* Supplement 59 (Summer 1987): 24-34.

Merton, Thomas. *New Seeds of Contemplation.* New York: New Directions Publishing Corporation, 1962.

Nouwen, Henri, J. M. *¡Gracias!* San Francisco: Harper & Row, 1983.

_____*The Way of the Heart.* New York: The Seabury Press, 1981.

Poling, James N., and Miller, Donald E. *Foundations for a Practical Theology of Ministry.* Nashville, Tenn.: Abingdon Press, 1985.

Rahner, Karl, S.J. *Foundations of Christian Faith.* New York: The Seabury Press, 1978.

_____*Opportunities for Faith.* New York: The Seabury Press, 1974.

_____*Theological Investigations.* vol. 3: *The Theology of the Spiritual Life.* Translated by Karl-H. and Boniface Kruger. Baltimore, Helicon Press, 1967. vol. VII: *Further Theology of the Spiritual Life I.* Translated by David Bourke. New York: Herder & Herder, 1971.

Robb, Paul V., S.J. "Conversion as a Human Experience." *Studies in the Spirituality of Jesuits* 14 (May 1982): 1-50.

Robson, Jill, and Lonsdale, David, eds. *Can Spirituality Be Taught?* London: Association of Centres of Adult Theological Association and British Council of Churches, 1988.

Shannon, William H. *Seeking the Face of God.* New York: Crossroad, 1988.

Smits, Kenneth, Capuchin. "Franciscan Living: an Ecology of Prayer, Community, and Ministry." *The New Round Table* 37 (Spring 1984): 73-108.

St. Louis, Donald. "The Ignatian Examen: A Method of Theological Reflection." *The Way,* Supplement no. 55. (Spring, 1986): 66-76.

Sobrino, Jon, S.J. *Christology at the Crossroads.* Translated by John Drury. Maryknoll: Orbis Books, 1978.

Synod of Bishops. *Justice in the World.* (Washington, D.C.: United States Catholic Conference, 1971.)

Teilhard de Chardin, Pierre. *The Divine Milieu.* New York: Harper & Row, 1960.

Theophane the Monk. *Tales of a Magic Monastery.* New York: Crossroad, 1981.

Tillard, J.M.R., O.P. *Dilemmas of Modern Religious Life.* Consecrated Life Studies. vol. 3. Wilmington, Delaware: Michael Glazier, Inc., 1984.

Tracy, David. *A Blessed Rage for Order.* New York: The Seabury Press, 1975.

_____ "The Foundations of Practical Theology." In *Practical Theology: The Emerging Field in Theology, Church, and World,* pp. 61-82. Edited by Don Browning, New York: Harper & Row, 1983.

Vatican Council II, 1962-1965. *The Documents of Vatican II.* Walter M. Abbott, General Editor; Joseph Gallagher, Translation Editor; New York: Guild Press, 1966.

Walsh, James, S.J. "Apostolic Religious Life: A Sea of Uncertainties." *Review for Religious* 44 (July / August, 1985): 552-65.

Westley, Dick. *A Theology of Presence.* Mystic, Ct.: Twenty-Third Publications, 1988.

Whitehead, James D., and Whitehead, Evelyn Eaton. *The Emerging Laity.* New York: Doubleday & Company, 1986.

_____ *Method in Ministry.* New York: The Seabury Press, 1980.

Young, William J., S.J., trans. *Finding God in All Things.* Essays in Ignatian Spirituality selected from *Christus.* Chicago: Henry Regnery Co., 1958.